Harry Potter

A HISTORY OF MAGIC

Harry Potter

A HISTORY OF MAGIC

THE OFFICIAL COMPANION TO THE BRITISH LIBRARY EXHIBITION AT THE

NEW-YORK HISTORICAL SOCIETY
MUSEUM & LIBRARY

ARTHUR A. LEVINE BOOKS
AN IMPRINT OF SCHOLASTIC INC.

This book is based on the British Library exhibition at the New-York Historical Society, *Harry Potter: A History of Magic.*

J.K. Rowling illustrations, images, manuscript pages, and Harry Potter quotes © J.K. Rowling
Foreword © 2018 by Louise Mirrer
Introduction by Julian Harrison © 2018 by British Library Board
Text © British Library Board
Text on pages 31, 54, 70-71, 92, 101, 122 (top), 134, 142, 148, 152, 158 (top), 163, 180, 186, 208, 210, 220, 228, 251-253, 256 © 2018 by New-York Historical Society
British Library images © British Library Board
Please also see picture credits on page 270.

Wizarding World is a trademark of Warner Bros. Entertainment Inc.
Wizarding World publishing rights © J.K. Rowling
Wizarding World characters, names, and related indicia are TM and © Warner Bros. Entertainment Inc. All rights reserved.

Library of Congress Cataloging-in-Publication Data available
ISBN 978-1-338-31150-1
10 9 8 7 6 5 4 3 2 1   18 19 20 21 22

Printed in China   62
First edition, October 2018
Book design by Rodrigo Corral Studio © Scholastic Inc.

CONTENTS

LOUISE MIRRER
President and CEO,
New-York Historical Society

FOREWORD

"History Matters" has long been the motto of the New-York Historical
Society, New York's first museum and distinguished research library,
founded in 1804. How true this motto rings with the launch of the
British Library's magnificent exhibition, *Harry Potter: A History of Magic*,
at New-York Historical in October 2018. At once drawing on the global
phenomenon of J.K. Rowling's Harry Potter novels and the traditions
of folklore and magic that underpin them, the exhibition shows, above
all, how art, artifacts, and documents of the past were indispensable to
one of our contemporary era's most creative minds. The exhibition also
underscores the importance of institutions such as the British Library and
New-York Historical, each a great repository of documents and ephemera
whose value and interest go well beyond the merely antiquarian. Rare
books, manuscripts, and magical objects from our two institutions, as
well as from US Harry Potter publisher Scholastic and other collections,
breathe new life into the annals of the distant past as they illuminate the
fascinating and more recent chapter begun with J.K. Rowling's books.

    The exhibition's opening at New-York Historical marks the 20th
anniversary of the US publication of *Harry Potter and the Sorcerer's Stone*,
a book that introduced an entire generation of Americans (including my
son, Malcolm) to the pleasures of reading. Among the great strengths of
the exhibition, and offering its own particular delights, is the chance for
these first-generation Harry Potter readers—and indeed all of the visitors
to the show—to experience a new and perhaps unexpected lens through
which to understand Harry Potter's world. At New-York Historical, we are
glad to be able to showcase in New York some treasures from our library

and museum which were not on view in London last year, including John James Audubon's original watercolor of the Snowy Owl (recalling Harry's pet owl, Hedwig); an original printing of Cotton Mather's *The Wonders of the Invisible World*, the minister's defense of his role in the infamous Salem witch trials; and a manuscript notebook from the 1720s with an unidentified navigator's notations charting the nighttime sky, including the constellations that inspired the name of Sirius Black and other Harry Potter characters. At the same time, we could not be more thrilled than to display the tremendous materials that were a part of the British Library exhibition in 2017 and are on loan to us.

It is through exhibitions such as *Harry Potter: A History of Magic* that great collections such as those that reside at the British Library and New-York Historical are able to enjoy a broad appeal. Still, this can only happen successfully when these collections are treated with the utmost respect, artistry, and intellect by talented and highly skilled women and men. We are grateful to our colleagues at the British Library, above all to Roly Keating, Jamie Andrews, Shona Connechen, and exhibition curators Julian Harrison, Alexander Lock, Tanya Kirk, and Joanna Norledge for their generous collaboration with us; as well as Ellie Berger, Emily Clement, Arthur Levine, David Saylor, Rachel Coun, Lizette Serrano, Charisse Meloto, and Kris Moran at Scholastic who worked to bring this exhibition and book to splendid fruition. We are also indebted to the local institutions whose loans have greatly enhanced the New York presentation: American Museum of Natural History, Beinecke Rare Book & Manuscript Library at Yale University, Brooklyn Museum, The Explorers Club, Metropolitan Museum of Art, and New York Botanical Garden. At New-York Historical, Margi Hofer, Gerhard Schlanzky, Cristian Petru Panaite, Jennifer Schantz, Emily Croll, Ines Aslan, and many other colleagues have contributed in ways too numerous to denominate. Cristian Petru Panaite and Margi Hofer, along with Rebecca Klassen, Marilyn Kushner, Nicole Mahoney, Roberta Olson, and Edward O'Reilly, made important contributions to this volume, as did New-York Historical trustee Agnes Hsu-Tang. I always reserve my greatest gratitude for New-York Historical's dedicated and generous Trustees, led by Chair Pam Schafler. Many thanks to all!

ROY DE DENIER

TENPERANCE

IVSTICE

LERMITE

LA PAPESSE

IIX

CAVALLIER DE BASTON

REYNE DE BASTON

ROY DE BASTON

LE PAPE

JULIAN HARRISON
British Library, Lead Curator
Harry Potter: A History Of Magic

INTRODUCTION

J.K. Rowling's Harry Potter novels are a global phenomenon. The stories have sold millions of copies worldwide, have been translated into dozens of languages, and inspired countless readers, young and old. But how many of those readers have paused to reflect on the magical traditions that lie at the heart of Harry Potter's world?

Harry Potter: A History of Magic is the first major exhibition to explore this rich and diverse aspect of J.K. Rowling's stories. From ancient amulets to medieval mandrakes, from unicorns (they really did exist) to bubbling cauldrons, there are often historical and mythological antecedents for the characters and scenes in the Harry Potter series. The exhibition strives to tell some of these stories and to celebrate the inspiration behind J.K. Rowling's own spellbinding creations.

The exhibition features many precious artifacts relating to the Harry Potter books and magic through the ages. First and foremost are items associated with J.K. Rowling. These include fascinating early drafts of *Harry Potter and the Sorcerer's Stone* and *Harry Potter and the Deathly Hallows*; original drawings by the author; and intricately worked-out plot plans for *Harry Potter and the Order of the Phoenix*. Each and every one of these treasures bears testament to the author's creativity and craftsmanship, and to the enduring appeal of the world she invented.

We are also delighted to showcase some of the original artwork of the artists Jim Kay, Mary GrandPré, Brian Selznick, and Olivia Lomenech Gill. Jim Kay has been commissioned to create fully illustrated editions of the Harry Potter novels, the first three of which have already been published to widespread international acclaim. Mary GrandPré is the illustrator of the iconic original American book jackets, giving US readers their first look at Harry. Brian Selznick has designed brand-new covers for the books in celebration of the 20th anniversary of *Harry Potter and the Sorcerer's*

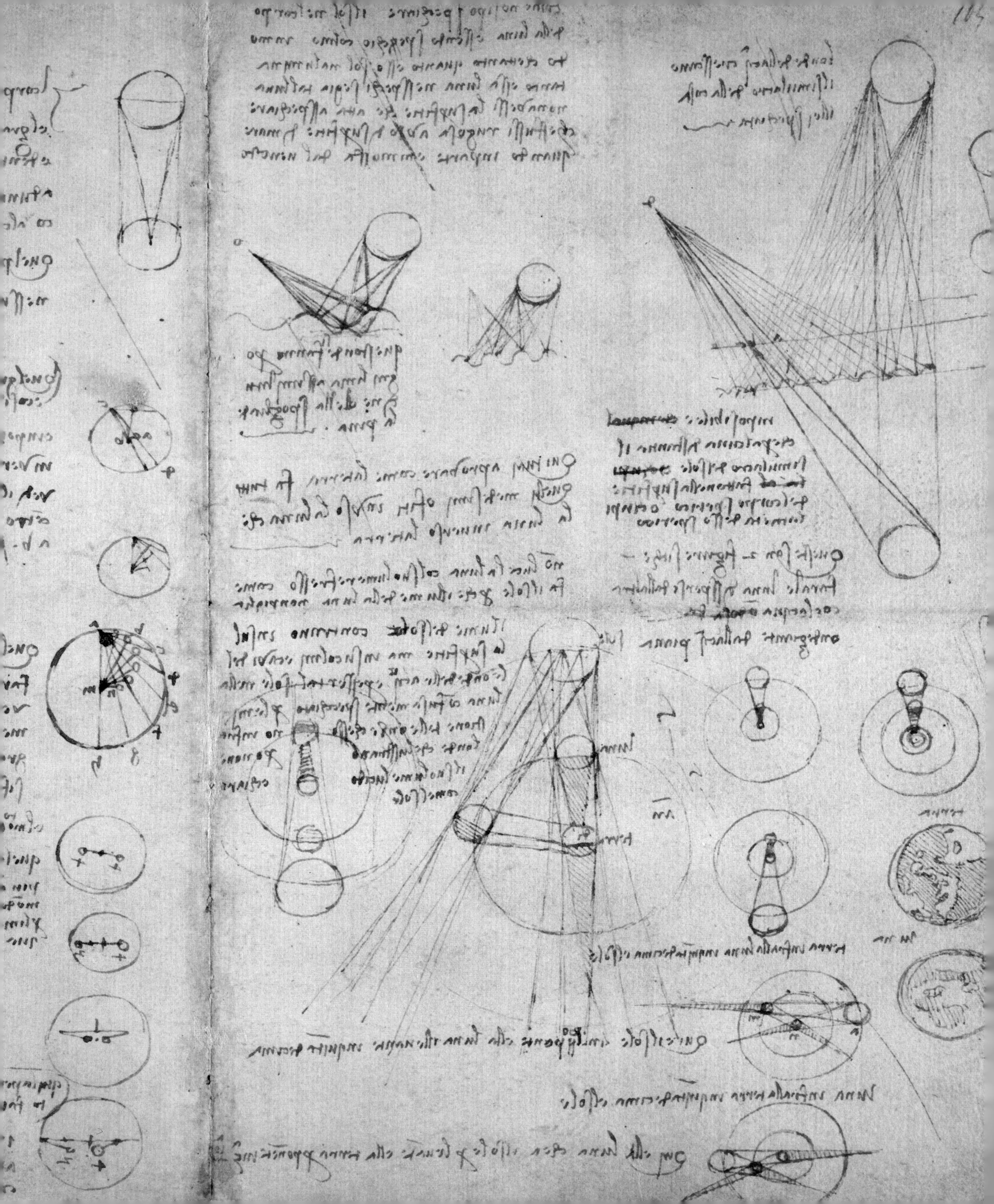

Stone in the United States, while Olivia Lomenech Gill is the artist of the illustrated edition of *Fantastic Beasts and Where to Find Them*. We are extremely grateful to all four for their generous involvement and support.

It is an equal pleasure to present items from the British Library's own unrivaled collections, many of which have never previously been considered in this wider, magical context. On display are Greek papyri, Ethiopian talismans, Chinese herbals, French phoenixes, and Thai horoscopes. Harry Potter fans can pore over Leonardo da Vinci's notebook, marvel at the Dunhuang Star Atlas, and gaze in amazement at the alchemist in the *Splendor Solis*. Visitors to New York will also be able to see a number of astonishing artifacts from the New-York Historical Society, foremost among which is the original watercolor of the Snowy Owl for Audubon's *Birds of America*, made in 1829. To complement these objects, we are also thrilled to have secured some amazing loans from a number of institutions and private individuals.

Harry Potter: A History of Magic is framed around some of the subjects studied at Hogwarts School of Witchcraft and Wizardry. There is Potions (and its more advanced cousin, Alchemy), Herbology, Charms, Astronomy, Divination, Defense Against the Dark Arts, and Care of Magical Creatures. Focusing on each of these subjects has enabled the exhibition curators to delve deeper into the theme of enchantment through the ages. Potion-making, fortune-telling, harvesting herbs and spells to make you invisible all make an appearance. In the process, we have uncovered intriguing facts about many of the exhibits. Did you know, for example, that Leonardo da Vinci believed that the Sun rotated around the Earth? Were you aware that the "Abracadabra" charm first originated as a cure for malaria? How many people knew that some unicorns had two horns? Some of these facts, quite frankly, border on the absurd—according to *The Old Egyptian Fortune-Teller's Last Legacy*, which we examine in Divination, "a mole on the buttock denotes honor to a man and riches to a woman."

The Harry Potter stories are rooted in centuries of popular tradition. Predicting the future, for instance, has a long history. One of the oldest items in the exhibition is a Chinese oracle bone, on loan from the Metropolitan Museum of Art. These ancient bones can date back as far as 1600 B.C.E., and were used for a divination ritual at the court of the Shang Dynasty. Such artifacts were known historically as "dragon bones," emphasizing their magical qualities.

The ancient art of alchemy is at the heart of the first story, *Harry Potter and the Sorcerer's Stone*. In that book, the mysterious Stone in question had been taken in secret to Hogwarts School, where it was being guarded by a monstrous three-headed dog named Fluffy and a series of protective spells placed upon it by the teachers. It was Hermione Granger who was the first to realize the significance of a certain Nicolas Flamel. Having spent several frustrating weeks with Harry and Ron Weasley in the library, she suddenly pulled out an old book that she had put aside for a bit of light reading.

> *"Nicolas Flamel," she whispered dramatically, "is the only known maker of the Sorcerer's Stone!"*

According to this ancient tome, Flamel was a noted alchemist and opera-lover, aged 665, who was living quietly in Devon with his wife, Perenelle. What readers of the Harry Potter stories may not have realized is that Flamel was a real person, a wealthy landlord who lived in medieval Paris, where he died in 1418. One of the star items in the exhibition is the actual headstone that marked the real Flamel's tomb, on loan from the Musée national du Moyen Âge in Paris.

Firenze the centaur was another to play a significant part in *Harry Potter and the Sorcerer's Stone*, saving Harry from danger in the Forbidden Forest before going on to teach Divination at Hogwarts in the later books. In Greek mythology, Chiron was the greatest of all centaurs, renowned as a physician and astrologer. According to a medieval herbal in our exhibition, the plants known as *Centauria major* and *Centauria minor* (greater and lesser centaury) were named after Chiron. He is shown in that manuscript handing over these plants to Asclepius, the god of medicine and healing. Centaury was renowned as a remedy for snakebite. Fans of Harry Potter will also be familiar with Sirius Black, Harry's godfather. Many of J.K. Rowling's characters are named after stars and constellations, and our exhibition features a medieval illustration of the constellation Canis Major, in which is found the Dog Star, also known as Sirius, the brightest star in the night sky.

Witches and wizards have long been associated with cauldrons and broomsticks. Included in the exhibition is the first printed image of witches with a cauldron, found in a book published in Germany in 1489. This illustration shows two elderly women placing a snake and a cockerel into a large cauldron, in a bid to summon up a hailstorm. Popular perceptions of witches as ugly, haggard, and demonic can ultimately be traced to this highly influential publication. One of the weirdest objects on display is a real witch's cauldron owned by the Museum of Witchcraft and Magic in Boscastle, England. The cauldron in question reportedly exploded when a group of witches were brewing a potion on the beach (think Neville Longbottom); the inside is now coated with a thick, tarry residue.

Every witch or wizard, so we have always been led to believe, should be able to fly on a broomstick. As Kennilworthy Whisp noted in *Quidditch Through the Ages*, "No Muggle illustration of a witch is complete without a broom." We are very happy to be showing in our exhibition a traditional witch's broomstick with an elaborately colored handle. Its former owner, Olga Hunt of Manaton in Devon, used this broomstick for magical purposes—on a Full Moon she is said to have leaped around Haytor Rocks on Dartmoor, much to the alarm of courting couples and campers. There is also a little book entitled *The History of the Lancashire Witches*, describing that English county as "famous for witches and the very strange pranks they have played." Alongside a picture of a jolly witch mounting a broomstick, the anonymous author declares, "Lancashire witches chiefly divert themselves in merriment and sport" and are "more sociable than any others."

Harry Potter fans will be familiar with the hazardous properties of mandrakes. According to medieval herbals, mandrakes could cure headaches, earache, and insanity, but their roots grew in human form and would shriek when torn. A 15th-century British Library manuscript shows the approved way to harvest that plant, by attaching one end of a cord to the plant and the other to a dog. The dog would be encouraged to move forward by sounding a horn or enticing it with meat, dragging the mandrake with it. There were a number of comparable drawings that we could have shown alongside this manuscript, but we plumped eventually for a 14th-century illustrated herbal, containing an Arabic translation of the writings of Pedanius Dioscorides, a physician in the Roman army. Dioscorides was one of the first to distinguish between the male and female mandrake (or maybe we should rename them the "mandrake" and the "womandrake"). Sadly for the romanticists among us, modern science now dictates that this identification is incorrect—there is more than one mandrake species native to the Mediterranean, rather than two separate sexes of the same plant.

This exhibition is alive with tales of human enterprise and endeavor. Elizabeth Blackwell illustrated, engraved, and hand-colored her *Curious Herbal* to raise funds to have her husband, Alexander, released from a debtors' prison. Alexander Blackwell assisted by identifying the plants she had drawn at Chelsea Physic Garden in London, until such time as she had absolved the debt. Once released he repaid his wife's kindness by leaving for Sweden, entering the service of King Frederick I, and getting himself executed for his involvement in a political conspiracy. The poignant copy of *A Curious Herbal* on display in *Harry Potter: A History of Magic* has been annotated in Elizabeth Blackwell's own hand.

Some magical advice dispensed over the centuries now seems rather quaint in a modern context. Quintus Serenus Sammonicus, physician to the Emperor Caracalla, recommended that the "Abracadabra" charm should be worn as an amulet around the neck, fixed with either flax, coral stones, or the fat of a lion. An Ethiopian charm for changing oneself into various animals, and for which there is no counter-charm, reads as follows:

> *With red ink, write these secret names on a piece of white silk. To transform yourself into a lion, tie the silk to your head; to become a python, tie it on your arm; to turn into an eagle, tie it on your shoulder.*

Magical creatures abound in the Harry Potter novels. Many of these fantastic beasts are J.K. Rowling's own creations, but others have illustrious precedents. Did you know that the French author Guy de la Garde devoted an entire study to the phoenix, entitled *L'Histoire et description du Phoenix*? The British Library's copy of this book is printed on vellum and contains a hand-colored picture of a phoenix emerging from a burning tree. A 13th-century bestiary also describes the "Fenix" in great detail. According to that manuscript, this mythical bird is so called because its color is "Phoenician purple," it is native to Arabia, and it can live for 500 years. In old age, the phoenix is said to create its own funeral pyre from branches and leaves, before fanning the flames with its own wings, in order to be consumed by the fire. After the ninth day, it rises again from the ashes.

In the second task of the Triwizard Tournament, relayed in *Harry Potter and the Goblet of Fire*, Harry encountered a choir of merpeople in the black lake at Hogwarts. Merpeople were also once intended to feature at the beginning of *Harry Potter and the Chamber of Secrets*, before the author had a change of mind. In a draft chapter subsequently rewritten by J.K. Rowling, the Ford Anglia flown by Ron and Harry originally crashed into the lake rather than into the Whomping Willow, leading them to see their first mermaid:

> *Her lower body was a great, scaly fishtail the color of gun-metal; ropes of shells and pebbles hung about her neck; her skin was a pale, silvery grey and her eyes, flashing in the headlights, looked dark and threatening.*

This description, although never published, echoes historical accounts of mermaids and mermen, creatures that were renowned, somewhat sinisterly, for luring people into the sea. On loan from the Horniman Museum in London is a specimen of a "real" merman, with large staring eyes and protruding teeth. In actual fact it is a fake. Scientific analysis

18

μονόκερως.

† περὶ ΜΟΝΟΚΕΡΩΤΟΣ :†

μονόκερως θὴρ πόλιν δοῖς ἐρέθη.
δεινός μὲν ἰδεῖν, εἰ δὲ λὰξ ἐπιπατέ6ι,
Σαρὶ μαχητής. ἢ δὲ κέντας ἐνδάκοι,
μόλις ἰαθὰ δ' ἃ φυᾶς χειρουργία.
πῦ σει πέρη δὲ τῷ φορὰν σβιν δάζου.
Σβάλυ δὲ πυκνὰ τὸν κορυφᾶον λόφου,
ἀλκῇ δ' μαχρῷ, ἢ φθορᾶς πλῆρες κέας
ὁ δ' ἀλκμὰν ἐκπεφυκὸς ὀφρύων.

the vertue of this experiment. So be yt, amen.

Afterwards psume the place wyth suche psumes, as shalbe appoynted in that chapter; sprincle yt also wyth water; and yff yt be necessary to make a sprincle, let suche an one be made as ys appoynted, as towching the same. If any other ceremonyes be required in this experiment doe them. when all these bee fynished, say thy coniuration, wyth thy dust doth searche the, and at the ende therof say.
Pater noster, Revax, Terson, Syletin, J adiure you by the holy name Joth, he, Vau, wch is wrytten wth 12. letters that by this present experiment we may see the truthe; Ja, Ja, Ja, ya, yah, cause thes spyrittes to showe vs our desyre. J coniure yow aforenamed spyrittes, by all that is aforesayde, and by hym to whom all creatures doe obay, that ymmediatly you showe vs the thing that we requyre; or elles hym that toke yt awaye. If yt to doe this experyment, yt be requisite, to write letters and figures, they ar to bee wrytten, as ys prescribed in the stronde booke; note that bye whatsoeuer meanes, experymentes for thefte arr made or done, requir yt ys, that there bee other experymentes besides this, as ys aboue say

Howe experymentes to be invysible must bee prepared, Cap. J.

Yff thou wylt haue an experiment to bee invysible, yff yt ys be required to write thy experiment, then write yt all in vyrgyn parchmente, and wyth pen and ynke, as shalbe appoynted in the chapter of pen and ynke, yff furdermore a coniuration be requyred, then before the coniuration say priuyly as followethe.
Stabbon, Asen, Gabellum, Saneney, Noty, Enobal, Labourem, Balametem, Balnon, Tygumel, Millegaly, Junneis, Hearma, Hamorache, yesa, Seya, Senoy, Henri Barucatha, Acavaras, Taracub, Bucaral, Caramy by the mercy whiche you beare towardes mann kynde, make me to be invysible; afterward make yor invocations, and yff you must mak

shows that its head was made by wrapping bundles of fiber around a stick of wood, coated with clay and then covered with papier-mâché; the jaws and tail were taken from a fish.

No exhibition about the world of Harry Potter would be complete without mentioning the most magical of mythical creatures, the unicorn. Unicorns—and unicorn blood—played a key part in Voldemort's continued survival in *Harry Potter and the Sorcerer's Stone*. The blood, hair, and horn of the unicorn have long been supposed to have medicinal proportion, according to medieval folklore. In mythology, the creature came in all shapes and sizes. A poem by the Byzantine writer Manuel Philes described the unicorn as a wild beast with the tail of a boar and a lion's mouth, while Pierre Pomet's *Histoire générale des Drogues* illustrated five species, including one, somewhat ironically, with two horns, known as the pirassoipi.

When I discover a beautifully imagined basilisk that has been hidden for centuries inside the pages of a bestiary, carefully unfurl an illuminated scroll that promises to reveal the secrets of the Philosopher's Stone, or breathe in the earthy pages of a centuries-old herbal, my connection to our magical past becomes tangible and real. Now I invite you to share in this rare enchantment. Many treasures await—whether you are curled up on the sofa with this book upon your lap or exploring the exhibition at the New-York Historical Society. As you gaze at the astonishing collection of artifacts in *Harry Potter: A History of Magic*, we hope you will be spellbound too.

P.S. You were wondering, of course, how to make yourself invisible. According to one 17th-century manuscript entitled *The Book of King Solomon Called The Key of Knowledge*, you simply have to recite the following words. Go ahead and try, but please don't blame us if the charm doesn't work!

Stabbon, Asen, Gabellum, Saneney, Noty, Enobal, Labonerem, Balametem, Balnon, Tygumel, Millegaly, Juneneis, Hearma, Hamorache, Yesa, Seya, Senoy, Henen, Barucatha, Acararas, Taracub, Bucarat, Caramy, by the mercy whitch you beare towardes mann kynde, make me to be invysible.

CHAPTER 1

the

JOURNEY

HARRY LOOKED UP INTO THE FIERCE, WILD, SHADOWY FACE AND SAW THAT THE BEETLE EYES WERE CRINKLED IN A SMILE. "LAS' TIME I SAW YOU, YOU WAS ONLY A BABY," SAID THE GIANT. "YEH LOOK A LOT LIKE YER DAD, BUT YEH'VE GOT YER MUM'S EYES."

—HARRY POTTER AND THE SORCERER'S STONE

THE BOY WHO LIVED

In this preparatory sketch by Jim Kay, Harry Potter is shown with his glasses taped up at the bridge and dark hair that just never *would* lie flat. He looks askance to the side with a cheeky glint in his eyes, reminiscent of his father's mischievous nature. At this stage, no color has been added to the image because Kay often digitally layers color over the original drawing—we cannot see the green color of Harry's eyes, a reminder of his mother, Lily. Harry Potter's youth and unworldliness at the beginning of the story is captured perfectly in this image, but it also looks like he may be the possessor of a wonderful secret. Kay's sketch invites us to reflect on the development of Harry's character throughout the books, from the wide-eyed child to the brave young man who stands up against Lord Voldemort.

"Jim Kay's portrait brings to life a young boy who seems both innocent and fragile. His large, expressive eyes, however, suggest a depth of character hidden beneath the surface. We get the feeling that there is a lot more about Harry Potter for us to discover . . ."

JOANNA NORLEDGE
Curator

◀

PORTRAIT OF HARRY POTTER BY JIM KAY
Bloomsbury

Synopsis

Harry Potter lives with his aunt, uncle and cousin because his parents died in a car-crash - or so he has always been told. The Dursleys don't like Harry asking questions; in fact, they don't seem to like anything about him, especially the very odd things that keep happening around him (which Harry himself can't explain).

The Dursleys' greatest fear is that Harry will discover the truth about himself, so when letters start arriving for him near his eleventh birthday, he isn't allowed to read them. However, the Dursleys aren't dealing with an ordinary postman, and at midnight on Harry's birthday the gigantic Rubeus Hagrid breaks down the door to make sure Harry gets to read his post at last. Ignoring the horrified Dursleys, Hagrid informs Harry that he is a wizard, and the letter he gives Harry explains that he is expected at Hogwarts School of Witchcraft and Wizardry in a month's time.

To the Dursleys' fury, Hagrid also reveals the truth about Harry's past. Harry did not receive the scar on his forehead in a car-crash; it is really the mark of the great dark sorcerer Voldemort, who killed Harry's mother and father but mysteriously couldn't kill him, even though he was a baby at the time. Harry is famous among the witches and wizards who live in secret all over the country because Harry's miraculous survival marked Voldemort's downfall.

So Harry, who has never had friends or family worth the name, sets off for a new life in the wizarding world. He takes a trip to London with Hagrid to buy his Hogwarts equipment (robes, wand, cauldron, beginners' draft and potion kit) and shortly afterwards, sets off for Hogwarts from Kings Cross Station (platform nine and three quarters) to follow in his parents' footsteps.

Harry makes friends with Ronald Weasley (sixth in his family to go to Hogwarts and tired of having to use second-hand spellbooks) and Hermione Granger (cleverest girl in the year and the only person in the class to know all the uses of dragon's blood). Together, they have their first lessons in magic - astonomy up on the tallest tower at two in the morning, herbology out in the greenhouses where the mandrakes and wolfsbane are kept, potions down in the dungeons with the loathsome Severus Snape. Harry, Ron and Hermione discover the school's secret passageways, learn how to deal with Peeves the poltergeist and how to tackle an angry mountain troll: best of all, Harry becomes a star player at Quidditch (wizard football played on broomsticks).

What interests Harry and his friends most, though, is why the corridor on the third floor is so heavily guarded. Following up a clue dropped by Hagrid (who, when he is not delivering letters, is Hogwarts' gamekeeper), they discover that the only Philosopher's Stone in existance is being kept at Hogwarts, a stone with powers to give limitless wealth and eternal life. Harry, Ron and Hermione seem to be the only people who have realised that Snape the potions master is planning to steal the stone - and what terrible things it could do in the wrong hands. For the Philospher's Stone is all that is needed to bring Voldemort back to full strength and power... it seems Harry has come to Hogwarts to meet his parents' killer face to face - with no idea how he survived last time...

◄ ▲

SYNOPSIS OF *HARRY POTTER AND THE PHILOSOPHER'S STONE* BY J.K. ROWLING (1995)
J.K. Rowling

THE AUTHOR'S SYNOPSIS

This is the original synopsis of the first Harry Potter book, typed to accompany the opening chapters of *Harry Potter and the Philosopher's Stone* (later published as *Harry Potter and the Sorcerer's Stone* in the US) and circulated among prospective agents and publishers. With folded corners, tea stains, and crumpled grip marks at the bottom, it is a document that has clearly been read and handled a great deal. From the very beginning, the lessons at Hogwarts were part of what makes Harry Potter's world so captivating. In just a few short lines, J.K. Rowling makes learning magic sound like amazing fun. Who wouldn't want to study Astronomy "in the tallest tower at two in the morning" and Herbology in the greenhouses "where the mandrake and wolfsbane are kept"?

"POSSIBLY ONE OF THE BEST BOOKS AN 8/9 YEAR OLD COULD READ"

Prior to being accepted for publication in the UK by Bloomsbury, the manuscript of *Harry Potter and the Philosopher's Stone* was famously offered to some eight publishers, all of whom rejected it. Nigel Newton, founder and Chief Executive of Bloomsbury, took the manuscript home and gave it to his eight-year-old daughter, Alice. Alice read the chapters, which went as far as Diagon Alley, and then gave her verdict, as preserved in this charming note. For long after she pestered her father to bring home the remainder of the manuscript. Alice's intervention was crucial: At the following day's acquisitions meeting, Newton approved editor Barry Cunningham's proposal that *The Philosopher's Stone* be published by Bloomsbury, leading to what is widely regarded as the most successful venture in children's publishing history.

The excitment in this book made me Feel warm inside. I think it is possibly one of the best books an 8/9 yearold could read

▲ READER'S REPORT OF ALICE NEWTON, AGED EIGHT, ON *HARRY POTTER AND THE PHILOSOPHER'S STONE*
Nigel Newton (Chief Executive, Bloomsbury Publishing Plc)

▶

DRAWING OF HARRY POTTER AND THE DURSLEYS BY J.K. ROWLING (1991)
J.K. Rowling

Fig 1: Harry Potter & the Dursleys

HARRY POTTER AND THE DURSLEYS

Made several years before the publication of *The Philosopher's Stone*, this early drawing by J.K. Rowling makes it instantly clear that Harry does not belong in the Dursley family. The boy's baggy T-shirt emphasizes his frailty in comparison to his sturdier relatives. Dudley Dursley has been drawn with his arms folded in a permanent sulk and a large piggy nose that makes him appear particularly beastly. Uncle Vernon stands glaring behind, while Aunt Petunia protectively clasps her son's shoulder. Despite the misery he experienced living at Privet Drive, Harry is the only person who seems able to raise a smile.

ARTHUR A. LEVINE BOOKS
AN IMPRINT OF SCHOLASTIC PRESS

December 19, 1997

J.K. Rowling

███████████

███████████

███████████

Dear Joanne,

Greetings from the United States. I hope this letter finds you well, and intact after the holidays! I am looking forward (with some trepidation) to cooking Christmas dinner for 22 people, so the "intact" part is by no means assured for me! And since I'm Jewish, I then have Hanukkah *and* New Years to contend with. It's a lot of celebrating.

But speaking of celebrating: I hope you got the flowers and card I sent about the Smarties Prize. Everyone here was so pleased to hear that you'd won. I hope you've been able to savor the accolades!

We are gearing up for the American publication of your book. I'm scribbling away at catalog copy. We've hired a magnificent artist named Mary Grandpre to do the jacket and small spot illustrations for the chapter openings. The production department has gotten involved, and will be getting special uncoated paper for the jacket to give it a lovely, classic look (and which will make the art and the gold-stamped type we're planning, show up beautifully.) I can't wait to see it come together and to show it to you!

The marketing department is also coming up with plans for the promotion of the book, and they will eventually be in touch with you about your availability for interviews, your willingness to travel, etc.

I am also going over the manuscript to see if there are any places where an American audience might need a word or two of "translation" or explanation. Mostly my attitude about such things is to leave the text as/is unless I think there is a chance for complete incomprehension, or worse, a word that means something quite different in our versions of English (for instance, a "jumper" in the U.S. is a one-piece skirt-and-bib-with-suspenders that only a small girl would wear.) You should receive that manuscript with my questions early in the new year. (Don't worry – there won't be much to do!)

The one question I'd like to pose to you right now, Joanne, is how wedded you are to the title. When I edited the first installment of Philip Pullman's trilogy in the U.S. we changed the title to THE GOLDEN COMPASS (it was "Northern Lights" in the U.K.) which had a better reception here. Similarly, I'd like to propose an alternative title for the

███████████

███████████

first Harry Potter in the U.S. I like the sound of HARRY POTTER AND THE PHILOSOPHER'S STONE, but those who have heard it so far have found themselves misled into thinking the book will have an obscure, "philosophical" overtone. Chalk it up to idiot Americans, but I think we'd be better off *here* with a title that was a bit more playful (and easier to design)

What do you think of HARRY POTTER AND THE SCHOOL OF MAGIC. I think it has a nice ring to it; it evokes all the fun to come at Hogwarts without giving too much away, and it's a bit of a play on the sense of the word "school" (i.e. both an institution of learning, and a...philosophy as it were!)

Would you mull it over and give me your thoughts? I'll be looking forward to hearing from you, Joanne. I can't tell you how thrilled we are about HARRY.

All the best,

HARRY POTTER AND THE...

In December 1997, seven months prior to the publication of the first Harry Potter book in America, Scholastic editor Arthur Levine wrote the then relatively unknown British author J.K. Rowling to suggest an alternative title. Concerned that the *Philosopher's Stone* title didn't perfectly reflect the humor and the wide range of magic in the book (which contained far more than alchemy), Levine suggested changing the title to a more comprehensive and playful one: *Harry Potter and the School of Magic*. The choice did not feel right to the thirty-two-year-old author who countered with *Harry Potter and the Sorcerer's Stone*, a title that would launch Potter mania in the United States. The question of changing the title was resolved relatively quickly—in the letter from Rowling to Levine that appears on the next page (written about a month later), the *Sorcerer's Stone* title is already in place. Levine's School of Magic title idea did not disappear altogether. The French edition of *The Philosopher's Stone*, for example, was renamed *Harry Potter à L'école des Sorciers*.

29 January 1998

Dear Arthur,

And about bloody time, too, as we British say when the mood is upon us.

There are no less than three half-completed letters to you saved on the hard drive of this word-processor (Arthurs 1, 2 and 3), but I am determined that Arthur 4 will be the one that actually makes it across the Atlantic. Shall I bore you with the details of my unprecedently busy couple of months? Suffice it to say that between Christmas, moving house, a bout of seasonal laryngitus, various trips to London (Bloomsbury - the publishers, not the area), a mountain of mail and examining all the day nurseries in this part of town to see which lucky establishment gets my daughter next, I have had the sensation of running very fast up a downward-bound escalator. So, even though I've already thanked over the 'phone, may I say thanks in writing for the flowers you sent after I won the Smarties, which were beautiful, and I am truely ashamed that Arthur 1 never made it into the post box, because those thanks would have been on time.

I can't wait to see the artwork for Harry Potter and the *Sorcerer's* Stone, I'm really excited about it, in fact; I would have loved chapter illustrations in the British edition but I don't think the budget permitted.

Next week I'm off to London *again* because HP & the PS has been nominated for another award. These are publishers' awards, and I'm told the books are judged partly on how much of a stir they have made publicity-wise. So I'm busy practising my false smile for the author who beats me, and will be assuming the persona of a reserved, serious writer who is really much more comfortable out of the limelight.

Sorry, again, and thanks, again.

With best wishes for '98,

Jo   aka J. K. Rowling

PS Twenty two people for Christmas dinner? Are you *mad?* - sorry - crazy.

PPS Your edits for the Sorcerer's Stone have just arrived so stand by for Arthur 5.

◄

LETTER FROM
J.K. ROWLING TO
ARTHUR LEVINE
(JANUARY 29, 1998)
Scholastic

A SCARLET STEAM ENGINE WAS WAITING NEXT TO A PLATFORM PACKED WITH PEOPLE. A SIGN OVERHEAD SAID HOGWARTS EXPRESS, ELEVEN O'CLOCK.

—HARRY POTTER AND THE SORCERER'S STONE

THE HOGWARTS EXPRESS

The painting by Jim Kay on the next page is a preliminary version of the artwork featured on the front cover of the illustrated edition of *The Sorcerer's Stone*. It shows the busy platform nine and three-quarters at King's Cross as students board the Hogwarts Express at the beginning of term. Harry Potter is singled out, standing with his loaded trolley and Hedwig amidst the hustle and bustle of families seeing off their children. The Hogwarts Express has a fierce, fire-breathing animal head decorating the top of its chimney and a shining bright light—a small winged hog sits at the very front, a nod to the name of Hogwarts. This journey marked Harry's transition to the world of magic, away from the Muggle-realm of the Dursleys.

►

STUDY OF PLATFORM NINE AND
THREE-QUARTERS BY JIM KAY
Bloomsbury

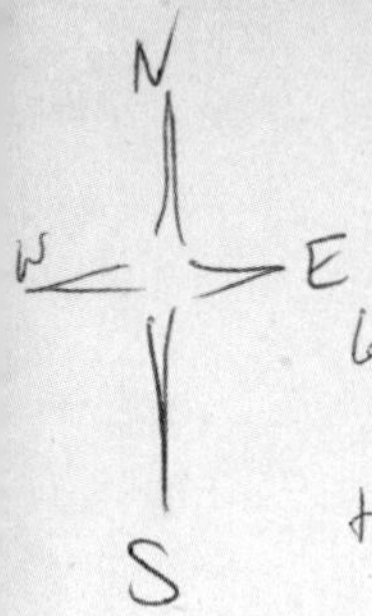

N
W ← → E
S

Forbidden forest is massive, stretches out of sight.
Southern approach over lake (castle stands on high cliff above lake/loch) — station's on other side)
To reach the school by stagecoach, go right round lake to front entrance at North.
Giant squid in Lake.
Seats all around Quidditch pitch — 3 long poles with hoops on at either end.
There can be other trees/bushes dotted around lawns but Whomping Willow must stand out.

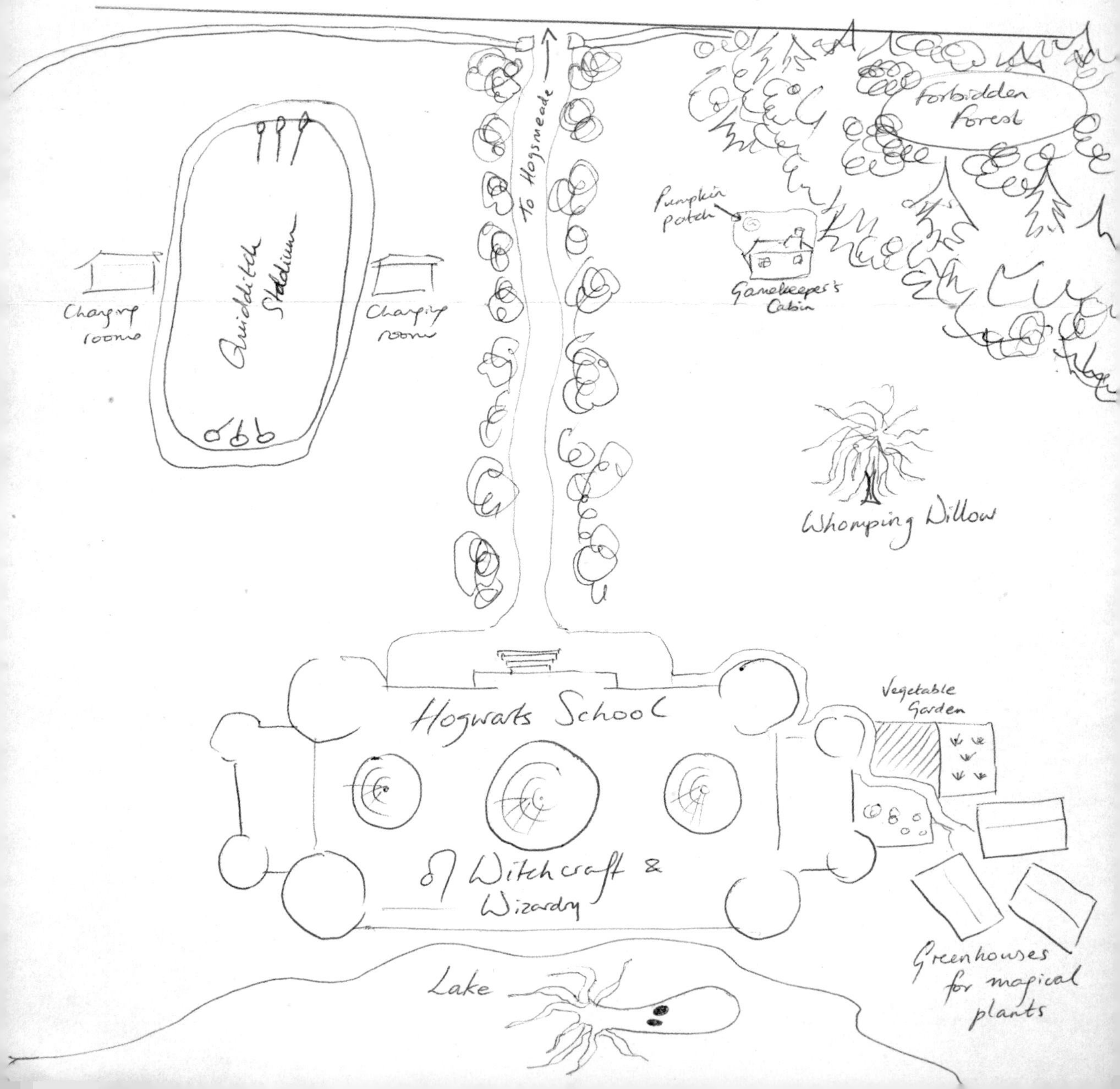

To Hogsmeade

Forbidden Forest

Quidditch Stadium

Charging rooms

Charging rooms

Pumpkin patch

Gamekeeper's Cabin

Whomping Willow

Hogwarts School
of Witchcraft & Wizardry

Vegetable Garden

Greenhouses for magical plants

Lake

This annotated sketch by J.K. Rowling shows the layout of Hogwarts School of Witchcraft and Wizardry, complete with the giant squid that lives in the lake. In an accompanying note addressed to her editor, J.K. Rowling stated, "This is the layout as I've always imagined it." The sketch provides a vital stepping-stone between the author's imagination and the world she has brought to life for so many readers. Note how the author insists that the "Whomping Willow must stand out," recognizing its significance in *The Chamber of Secrets* and *The Prisoner of Azkaban*.

SLIPPING AND STUMBLING, THEY FOLLOWED HAGRID DOWN WHAT SEEMED TO BE A STEEP, NARROW PATH [...] THERE WAS A LOUD "OOOOOH!" THE NARROW PATH HAD OPENED SUDDENLY ON TO THE EDGE OF A GREAT BLACK LAKE. PERCHED ATOP A HIGH MOUNTAIN ON THE OTHER SIDE, ITS WINDOWS SPARKLING IN THE STARRY SKY, WAS A VAST CASTLE WITH MANY TURRETS AND TOWERS.

—*HARRY POTTER AND THE SORCERER'S STONE*

◀

SKETCH OF HOGWARTS
BY J.K. ROWLING
Bloomsbury

PROFESSOR DUMBLEDORE

This portrait of Professor Albus Percival Wulfric Brian Dumbledore shows him gazing intently toward the right with bright blue eyes. A gargoyle vase sits on the table containing the dried branch of the plant of *Lunaria annua* or "honesty," known for its translucent seedpods. There is also a small flask, containing what might well be dragon's blood, referring to the wizard's achievement of discovering all twelve uses of the magical substance. Dumbledore's favorite sweets, lemon drops, feature as one of the passwords to his office. His knitting lies to one side, the orange wool curling across the table. Jim Kay's portrait captures the complexity of Dumbledore's personality—the powerful and serious wizard with a penchant for sweets and knitting.

AND THERE, IN THE CENTER OF THE HIGH TABLE, IN A LARGE GOLD CHAIR, SAT ALBUS DUMBLEDORE. HARRY RECOGNIZED HIM AT ONCE FROM THE CARD HE'D GOTTEN OUT OF THE CHOCOLATE FROG ON THE TRAIN. DUMBLEDORE'S SILVER HAIR WAS THE ONLY THING IN THE WHOLE HALL THAT SHONE AS BRIGHTLY AS THE GHOSTS.
—*HARRY POTTER AND THE SORCERER'S STONE*

"Albus means 'white' in Latin. Hagrid's first name, Rubeus, means 'red.' Harry's two father figures symbolically represent different stages of the alchemical process needed to create the Philosopher's Stone."
JOANNA NORLEDGE
Curator

▶
PORTRAIT OF PROFESSOR ALBUS DUMBLEDORE BY JIM KAY
Bloomsbury

PROF. MINERVA McGONAGALL

PROFESSOR McGONAGALL

Professor Minerva McGonagall is Deputy Headmistress, Head of Gryffindor House, and Transfiguration teacher at Hogwarts. Dressed in dark green with her hair drawn back in a severe bun, this portrait captures her intelligence and no-nonsense attitude. Her glasses sit low on her nose, ideal for peering piercingly at students. She is named "Minerva" after the Roman goddess of wisdom—her surname echoes the notoriously bad Scottish poet, William McGonagall. Giving such a highly capable and intelligent character the surname of a hopelessly awful poet is an example of the humor and wit employed throughout the world of Harry Potter.

A TALL, BLACK-HAIRED WITCH IN EMERALD-GREEN ROBES STOOD THERE. SHE HAD A VERY STERN FACE AND HARRY'S FIRST THOUGHT WAS THAT THIS WAS NOT SOMEONE TO CROSS.

—*HARRY POTTER AND THE SORCERER'S STONE*

◀

PORTRAIT OF PROFESSOR
MINERVA McGONAGALL
BY JIM KAY
Bloomsbury

THE TALES OF BEEDLE THE BARD

In the final Harry Potter novel, Dumbledore bequeaths his own copy of *The Tales of Beedle the Bard*, written in runes, to Hermione Granger. It contains several bedtime stories told widely in the magical world, equivalent to Muggle fairy tales such as those by Hans Christian Andersen or the Brothers Grimm. One particular story, "The Tale of the Three Brothers," plays a vital role in helping Harry, Hermione, and Ron uncover three legendary magical objects known as the Deathly Hallows—the Elder Wand, the Resurrection Stone, and the Invisibility Cloak. This copy of *Beedle the Bard* was handwritten and illustrated by J.K. Rowling and embellished with rhodochrosite stones, associated with love and balance. It was originally gifted to Barry Cunningham, who accepted the first Harry Potter book for publication in the UK by Bloomsbury.

WRITTEN IN RUNES

Runes are the characters of an early Germanic writing system, used in parts of northern Europe from roughly the 2nd century C.E. to the early 16th century. They have long been understood to possess magical qualities. The common Germanic root of the word "rune" is *run*, which meant "mystery" or "secrecy" in the languages—Old Norse, Old High German, Old English—that employed these characters. Although runes are no longer written today, their symbols are still commonly used in magic. Made from antler, these divination discs are inscribed with red runes, and are meant to be scattered and then interpreted.

▶
THE TALES OF BEEDLE THE BARD BY J.K. ROWLING
Private Owner

▼
RUNE ANTLER DISCS
The Museum of Witchcraft and Magic, Boscastle

The Tales of
Beedle the Bard
translated from the
original runes
by
JK Rowling

Babbitty Rabbitty
and her Cackling Stump

A long time ago, in a far
off land, there lived a foolish
King. She decided that he
alone should have the
power of magic.

CHAPTER **2**

POTIONS and

ALCHEMY

PROF. SEVERUS SNAPE

"I DON'T EXPECT YOU WILL REALLY UNDERSTAND THE BEAUTY OF THE SOFTLY SIMMERING CAULDRON WITH ITS SHIMMERING FUMES, THE DELICATE POWER OF LIQUIDS THAT CREEP THROUGH HUMAN VEINS, BEWITCHING THE MIND, ENSNARING THE SENSES. . . ."

—PROFESSOR SNAPE, *HARRY POTTER AND THE SORCERER'S STONE*

▲ PORTRAIT OF PROFESSOR
SEVERUS SNAPE BY JIM KAY
Bloomsbury

THE POTIONS MASTER

This formal portrait by Jim Kay captures the sneering Professor Snape that Harry so mistrusts in the first book, but the objects scattered in front of him hint at his complex character and his role in the stories.

1. The bottled mole signifies his role as a spy for the Order of the Phoenix.

2. Lilies of the valley by his hands repre-sent his enduring love for Harry's mother, Lily.

3. Scissors refer to Sectumsempra, the Dark Magic spell Snape had invented, and might also refer to the two halves of his identity as a double agent.

4. A snake pattern decorates his shirt, while a snake clasp pins his cloak at the neck. His green cravat and the tabletop echo the color of his house, Slytherin. J.K. Rowling has explained elsewhere that, in the novels, Dark Magic is often represented by the color green.

A LEAKY CAULDRON

Cauldrons are one of the most ancient and widely recognized symbols of magic in Western culture. Indeed, to be a *strioportius* (witch's cauldron carrier) was a punishable offense in 6th-century Salic law. All first-year students at Hogwarts were required to pack their own cauldron when attending school. This enchanted cooking pot is coated in a black, tarry substance. It exploded when some Cornish witches were concocting a powerful potion by the sea. The group had gathered to invoke a spirit. One account describes how, when "it was realized that the volume of the smoke was reaching unprecedented proportions . . . they lost their nerve and panicked and fled the spot as best they could."

HERMIONE THREW THE NEW INGREDIENTS INTO THE CAULDRON AND BEGAN TO STIR FEVERISHLY. "IT'LL BE READY IN A FORTNIGHT," SHE SAID HAPPILY.

—HARRY POTTER AND THE CHAMBER OF SECRETS

① Ocul. Cancr.—
"crabs' eyes"—stony
concretions taken
from the stomachs
of putrefied crayfish,
prescribed to aid
digestion!

② Sang. Draco.V.—
"Dragon's Blood," a
potent red resin that
is still widely used in
medicine, magic, art,
and alchemy

③ Vitriol. Coerul.—
copper sulphate

▲ A SET OF APOTHECARY
JARS (SPAIN?, 17TH OR
18TH CENTURY)
Science Museum

◀ AN EXPLODED
CAULDRON (ENGLAND,
MID-20TH CENTURY)
*The Museum of Witchcraft
and Magic, Boscastle*

▶ PRELIMINARY PENCIL
SKETCH OF POTIONS
BOTTLES BY JIM KAY
Bloomsbury

APOTHECARY JARS

As early as 1500 B.C.E., the ancient Egyptians
recognized that glass was an excellent vessel for
storing chemical substances—it is nonabsorbent
and will not adulterate the contents. These glass
apothecary jars used this ancient technology to store
a selection of medicinal ingredients.

▲
**ULRICH MOLITOR,
DE LANIIS ET
PHITONICIS
MULIERIBUS...
TRACTATUS
PULCHERRIMUS
(REUTLINGEN, 1489)**
British Library

"The woodcut illustration in this book was massively influential. The image of women gathered around a cauldron established a powerful visual iconography for witchcraft that has lasted for centuries. Not everybody can read words, but anyone can read a picture."

ALEXANDER LOCK
Curator

A POTIONS CLASS

This medieval book, *Ortus Sanitatis* ("The Garden of Health"), is the first printed encyclopedia of natural history, featuring sections devoted to plants, animals, birds, fish, and stones. In this hand-colored woodcut engraving we see a Potions master instructing a group of students. He is shown wearing an ermine-lined gray cloak, clutching a stick in his left hand, with his assistant before him holding open a book of recipes. It is questionable how much attention the students are paying to their teacher.

▶
JACOB MEYDENBACH,
ORTUS SANITATIS
(MAINZ, 1491)
British Library

FIRE BURN AND CAULDRON BUBBLE

Although the association of cauldrons with witches dates back to at least the 6th century, this motif did not gain widespread acceptance until *On Witches and Female Fortune-Tellers* was published in 1489. Ulrich Molitor's book is the earliest illustrated treatise on witchcraft and contains the first printed depiction of witches with a cauldron. This page shows two elderly women placing a snake and a rooster into a flaming pot in an attempt to summon a hailstorm. The book was so widely reproduced that it helped to consolidate modern impressions of how witches were supposed to behave.

"IT'S NOT EASY TER CATCH A UNICORN, THEY'RE POWERFUL MAGIC CREATURES. I NEVER KNEW ONE TER BE HURT BEFORE."

—RUBEUS HAGRID, *HARRY POTTER AND THE SORCERER'S STONE*

◄

A PHARMACY SIGN IN THE
SHAPE OF A UNICORN'S
HEAD (18TH CENTURY)
Science Museum

AN APOTHECARY'S SIGN

Throughout history, the blood, hair, and horns of unicorns were believed to possess powerful medicinal properties. Because of their rarity, they commanded very high prices. In *The Sorcerer's Stone*, Voldemort survives on unicorn blood, and potions are made from "silver unicorn horns" that in Diagon Alley cost "twenty-one Galleons." This 18th-century sign from an apothecary's shop features a very handsome unicorn. The expertly carved sign shows the prosperity of the apothecary and his ability to acquire precious and exotic cures. Although the ivory horn looks like it belongs to a genuine unicorn, this example is actually made from a narwhal's tusk. Known as the "unicorn of the sea," narwhal tusks were often sold and marketed in this way.

PREPPING POTION INGREDIENTS

The mortar and pestle, a bowl of wood or metal with a club-shaped instrument for grinding ingredients into a fine powder, was an essential tool of apothecaries and alchemists. Hogwarts students used mortars and pestles to prepare ingredients for potions. Typical of sets used in the US during the 19th century, this mortar and pestle is made of lathe-turned wood and was used by members of the Babcock family of Rhode Island, most likely for grinding herbs and spices. The metal herb grinder offered an even more efficient method: grasping the wooden handle with two hands and rolling the heavy, sharp-edged cast-iron wheel produced pulverized potion ingredients with minimal effort. This boat-shaped device may have been cast in the New Jersey iron foundry of Philadelphia pharmacist and entrepreneur Clayton Brown Rogers.

**MORTAR AND PESTLE
(UNITED STATES,
19TH CENTURY)**
New-York Historical Society
▼

▶ HERB GRINDER
(UNITED STATES,
19TH CENTURY)
New-York Historical Society

SNAPE PUT THEM ALL INTO PAIRS AND SET
THEM TO MIXING UP A SIMPLE POTION TO
CURE BOILS. HE SWEPT AROUND IN HIS
LONG BLACK CLOAK, WATCHING THEM WEIGH
DRIED NETTLES AND CRUSH SNAKE FANGS,
CRITICIZING ALMOST EVERYONE EXCEPT
MALFOY, WHOM HE SEEMED TO LIKE.

—*HARRY POTTER AND THE SORCERER'S STONE*

These two pages show annotations by J.K. Rowling and her editor on a typed draft of *Harry Potter and the Half-Blood Prince*. The action on the first page takes place in Professor Slughorn's class. The wizard presents a series of potions, which Hermione, naturally, is able to identify. The added text marked by an asterisk reveals the smells that Hermione finds attractive, including the scent of "new parchment." The second page is the draft of a scene in which Harry consults the Half-Blood Prince's copy of *Advanced Potion-Making* to find out how to brew more Felix Felicis.

▶

DRAFT OF
HARRY POTTER
AND THE HALF-
BLOOD PRINCE,
ANNOTATED BY
J.K. ROWLING
AND HER EDITOR
(CA. 2004-2005?)
Bloomsbury

'It's Veritaserum, a colourless, odourless potion that forces the drinker to tell the truth,' said Hermione.

'Very good, very good!' said Slughorn, beaming at her. 'Now, this one here is pretty well-known… featured in a few Ministry leaflets lately, too… who can -?'

Hermione's hand was fastest once more.

'It's Polyjuice Potion, sir,' she said.

Harry, too, had recognised the slow-bubbling, mud-like substance in the second cauldron, but did not resent Hermione getting the credit for answering the question; she, after all, was the one who had succeeded in making it, back in their second year.

'Excellent, excellent! Now, this one here… yes, my dear?' said Slughorn, now looking slightly bemused, as Hermione's hand punched the air again.

'It's Amortentia!'

'It is indeed. It seems almost foolish to ask,' said Slughorn, who was looking mightily impressed, 'but I assume you know what it does?'

'It's the most powerful love potion in the world!' said Hermione.

'Quite right! You recognised it, I suppose, by its distinctive mother-of-pearl sheen?'

'And the steam rising in characteristic spirals,' said Hermione. ✳

'May I ask your name, my dear?' *said Slughorn, ignoring these signs of embarrassment.*

'Hermione Granger, sir.'

'Granger? Granger? Can you possibly be related to Hector Dagworth-Granger, who founded the Most Extraordinary Society of Potioneers?'

'No, I don't think so, sir. I'm Muggle-born, you see.'

✳ 'and it's supposed to smell differently to each of us, according to what attracts us, and I can smell freshly-mown grass and new parchment and —'
But she turned slightly pink and did not complete the sentence

175

'How many times have we been through this?' she said wearily. 'There's a big difference between needing to use the room and wanting to see what Malfoy needs it for –'

'Harry might need the same thing as Malfoy and not know he needs it!' said Ron. 'Harry, if you took a bit of Felix, you might suddenly feel the same need as Malfoy –'

'Harry, don't go wasting the rest of that Potion! You'll need all the luck you can get if Dumbledore takes you along with him to destroy a,' she dropped her voice to a whisper, 'horcrux – so you just stop encouraging him to take a slug of Felix every time he wants something!' she added sternly to Ron.

'Couldn't we make some more?' Ron asked Harry, ignoring Hermione. 'It'd be great to have a stock of it... have a look in the book...'

Harry pulled his copy of *Advanced Potion-Making* out of his bag and looked up *Felix Felicis*.

'Blimey, it's seriously complicated,' he said, running an eye down the list of ingredients. 'And it takes six months... you've got to let it stew...'

'Dammit,' said Ron.

Harry was about to put his book away again when he noticed that the corner of a page turned down; turning to it, he saw the 'Sectumsempra' spell, captioned 'for Enemies,' that he had marked a few weeks previously. He had still not found out what it did, mainly because he did not want to test it around Hermione, but he was considering trying it out on McLaggen next time he came up behind him unawares.

The only person who was not particularly pleased to see Katie Bell back at school was Dean Thomas, because he would no longer be required to fill her place as Chaser. He took the blow stoically enough when Harry told him, merely grunting and

3

The Animal y^t bears y^e Bezoar
or y^e Bezoar Goat.

4

The Musk Goat.

THE BEZOAR GOAT

In his very first Potions lesson, Professor Snape asked Harry Potter, "where would you look if I told you to find me a bezoar?" Bezoars are a mass of undigested fiber formed in the stomach of animals, and were once believed to be an antidote to poison. They have been found in the guts of cows and even elephants, but mostly they come from the "bezoar goat." Bezoars were first introduced into medieval Europe by Arab physicians. Although doubts were sometimes cast over their properties, the demand continued well into the 18th century. Wealthy collectors spent considerable sums to acquire the best "stones," which were kept in elaborate cases. According to A *Compleat History of Druggs*, first published in French in 1694, the medicinal strength of the bezoar depended on the animal that produced it. "Bezoar Stones taken from Cows," for instance, "have nothing near the good Qualities" of the true bezoar goat. On the other hand, a mere two grains of "the Bezoar that is found in Apes" will have a far greater effect than that of a mere goat. In *The Half-Blood Prince*, Harry put his learning to good effect. In his copy of *Advanced Potion-Making*, Harry had noticed the instruction, "Just shove a bezoar down their throats." He did exactly that when Ron Weasley drank some poisoned mead, thereby saving his friend's life.

"There are lots of interesting stories and anecdotes about bezoars. Scrapings of the stone were swallowed in an attempt to cure a range of illnesses. Repelling poison may not have been such a stretch, as ingesting the stone would likely cause vomiting."

ALEXANDER LOCK
Curator

◄

PIERRE POMET,
A COMPLEAT HISTORY
OF DRUGGS, 2ND EDN
(LONDON, 1725)
British Library

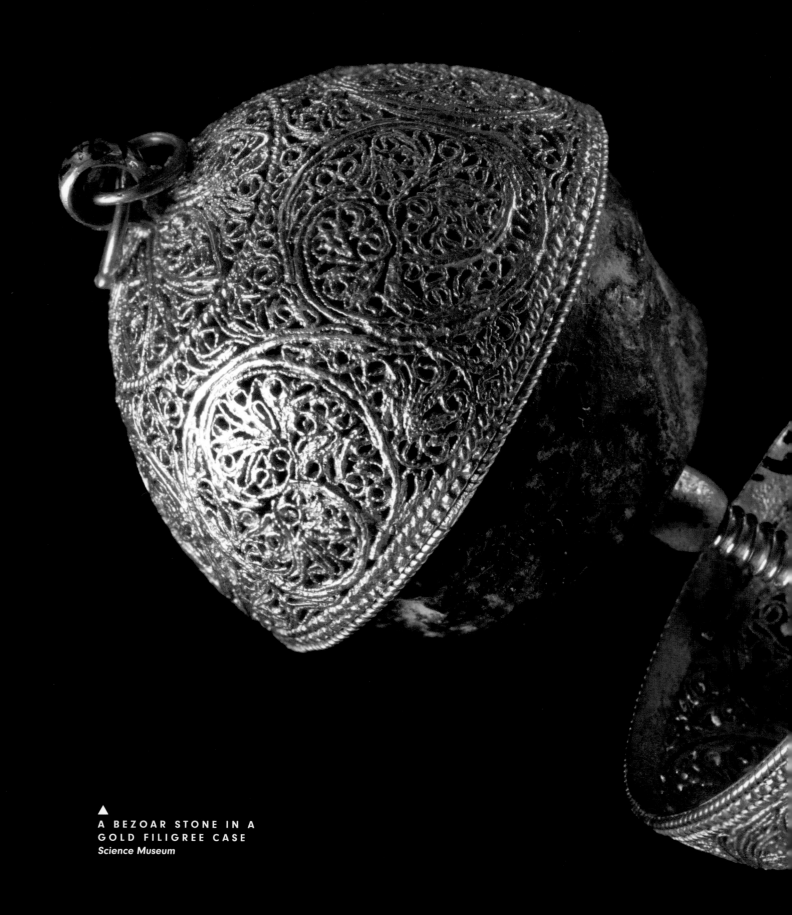

A BEZOAR STONE IN A
GOLD FILIGREE CASE
Science Museum

"BLIMEY, IT WAS LUCKY YOU THOUGHT OF A BEZOAR," SAID GEORGE IN A LOW VOICE.
"LUCKY THERE WAS ONE IN THE ROOM," SAID HARRY, WHO KEPT TURNING COLD AT THE THOUGHT OF WHAT WOULD HAVE HAPPENED IF HE HAD NOT BEEN ABLE TO LAY HANDS ON THE LITTLE STONE.

—*HARRY POTTER AND THE HALF-BLOOD PRINCE*

THE RIPLEY SCROLL

The Ripley Scroll is the name given to a mystical alchemical treatise that features a series of verses about the Elixir of Life. The scroll takes its name from George Ripley, a canon at Bridlington Priory in Yorkshire and a skilled alchemist. Ripley had reportedly studied alchemy in Italy and at the University of Louvain in modern-day Belgium. He subsequently wrote a book on how to make the Philosopher's Stone, known as *The Compound of Alchymy*. This manuscript is based on Ripley's teachings, and stretches almost six meters in length. It features beautiful illustrations of dragons, toads, and a winged bird captioned, "The Bede of Hermes is mi name, eting mi wines to make me tame." At the head of the scroll is a robed, bearded figure holding an alchemical vessel. Inside two figures can be seen lifting up the so-called "Book of Philosophy."

▲ ▼
**THE RIPLEY SCROLL
(ENGLAND, CA. 1570)**
Beinecke Rare Book and Manuscript Library, Yale University

"Very few people have seen the Ripley Scroll in its fullest extent, simply because it is such an enormous document. The manuscript in its entirety is full of symbolism—richly decorated with creatures and motifs that represent the alchemical process."

JULIAN HARRISON
Lead Curator

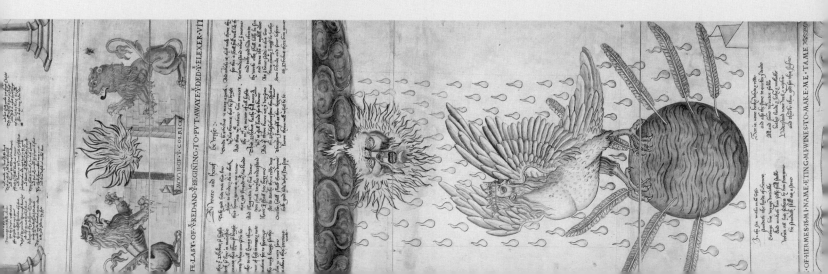

THE ANCIENT STUDY OF ALCHEMY
IS CONCERNED WITH MAKING THE
SORCERER'S STONE, A LEGENDARY
SUBSTANCE WITH ASTONISHING
POWERS. THE STONE WILL TRANSFORM
ANY METAL INTO PURE GOLD. IT ALSO
PRODUCES THE ELIXIR OF LIFE, WHICH
WILL MAKE THE DRINKER IMMORTAL.
—HARRY POTTER AND THE SORCERER'S STONE

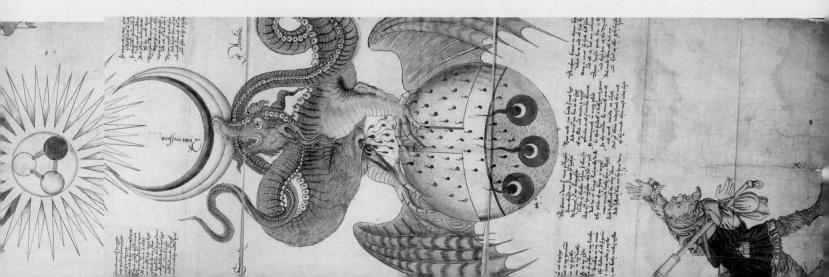

SPLENDOR SOLIS

Perhaps the most beautiful of all illuminated manuscripts about alchemy, this book contains the work known as *Splendor Solis* or "Splendor of the Sun." The authorship is unknown, but it has often been attributed in error to Salomon Trismosin, a man who claimed to have used the Philosopher's Stone to conquer old age. This page shows an alchemist holding a flask filled with a golden liquid. A black scroll emerges out of the flask, inscribed with the words "*Eamus quesitum quatuor elementorum naturas,*" Latin for "Let us ask the four elements of nature."

▲
**SPLENDOR SOLIS
(GERMANY, 1582)**
British Library

"The splendid gold border on this page is equally as impressive as the portrait in the center. The frame has been painstakingly decorated with pictures of flowers, birds, and animals—among them a peacock, a stag, and an owl."

JULIAN HARRISON
Lead Curator

BOOK OF THE
SEVEN CLIMES

Abū al-Qāsim Muhammad ibn Ahmad al-'Irāqī was an author of books on alchemy and magic, and lived in Egypt in the 13th century. His *Book of the Seven Climes* is the earliest known study focused wholly on alchemical illustrations. This picture was supposedly taken from a "Hidden Book" attributed to Hermes Trismegistus, a legendary sage-king of ancient Egypt, believed to have mastered the secrets of alchemy and recorded them in hieroglyphs on the walls of tombs. Al-'Irāqī gave each element an alchemical interpretation, but in fact this illustration holds no such meaning! Unbeknownst to al-'Irāqī, the picture actually depicts an ancient monument erected in memory of King Amenemhat II, who ruled Egypt around 1922–1878 B.C.E.

▲
ILLUSTRATION OF THE
ALCHEMICAL PROCESS, IN
ABŪ AL-QĀSIM AL-'IRĀQĪ,
*KITĀB AL-AQĀLĪM
AL-SAB'AH (BOOK OF
THE SEVEN CLIMES)*
(18TH CENTURY)
British Library

NICOLAS FLAMEL, ALCHEMIST

In *The Sorcerer's Stone*, Harry, Hermione, and Ron spent considerable time in the library at Hogwarts trying to identify a certain Nicolas Flamel. Eventually, Hermione pulled out an old book she had put aside for a bit of light reading. "'Nicolas Flamel,' she whispered dramatically, '*is the only known maker of the Sorcerer's Stone!*'" According to Hermione's book, Flamel was a noted alchemist and opera-lover, aged 665, who lived quietly in Devon with his wife, Perenelle. Eventually, he agreed with his friend Albus Dumbledore that the Sorcerer's Stone should be destroyed. Flamel and his wife had "enough Elixir stored to set their affairs in order" before finally being laid to rest.

In reality, Flamel spent his life in medieval Paris and was a landlord, sometimes said (incorrectly) to have been involved in the book trade. The watercolor illustration at right shows a memorial to the Holy Innocents commissioned by Nicolas and Perenelle, with the Flamels praying at the top beside two saints. At his reputed death in 1418, he was buried in the church of Saint-Jacques-de-la-Boucherie in Paris, his grave marked by a small tombstone showing Christ flanked by Saints Peter and Paul, along with the Sun and the Moon, and the deceased lying below the main inscription, carved in French.

Flamel's reputation as an alchemist derives ultimately from posthumous accounts of his life. According to these 16th- and 17th-century legends, Flamel had a prophetic dream that led him to discover a rare manuscript revealing the true composition of the Philosopher's Stone (known as the Sorcerer's Stone in the American editions of the Harry Potter novels). First published in Germany in 1735, the *Uraltes Chymisches Werck* ("Age-Old Chemical Work"), reputedly by the rabbi Abraham Eleazar, claimed to be a translation of this lost text. In the picture on page 59, a serpent and a crowned dragon form a circle, head-to-tail. This is a common alchemical illustration, which symbolizes the unification *of materia* (primary matter) with *spiritus universalis* (the universal spirit). This unification was considered essential in the creation of the Stone.

"Nicolas Flamel is a fascinating character— an intersection in history between myth, legend, and the magic of Harry Potter. Almost everything we knew about him was incorrect. The real Flamel wasn't an alchemist, yet after his death this fantastical story somehow rose up around his name."

JULIAN HARRISON
Lead Curator

▶
WATERCOLOR ILLUSTRATIONS FROM A MEMOIR OF NICOLAS FLAMEL AND HIS WIFE (FRANCE, 18TH CENTURY)
British Library

Feu nicolas flamel iadiz escri
uain a laissie par son testament a
leuure de cette eglise certaines
rentes et maisons quil auoit
acquestees et achatees a son vi
uant pour faire certain seruice
diuin et distribucions dargent
chascun an par aumosne tou
chans les quinze vins lostel di
eu et autres eglises et hospitaux
a paris. Soit prie po les trespasse

Domine deus in tua misericordia speraui

De terre suis venus et en terre retourne
Lame rens a toy ihu qui les peche pardonne

"TO ONE AS YOUNG AS YOU, I'M SURE IT SEEMS INCREDIBLE, BUT TO NICOLAS AND PERENELLE, IT REALLY IS LIKE GOING TO BED AFTER A VERY, VERY LONG DAY. AFTER ALL, TO THE WELL-ORGANIZED MIND, DEATH IS BUT THE NEXT GREAT ADVENTURE."

—PROFESSOR DUMBLEDORE, *HARRY POTTER AND THE SORCERER'S STONE*

◄

TOMBSTONE OF NICOLAS FLAMEL (PARIS, 15TH CENTURY)
Musée national du Moyen Âge, Paris

►

R. ABRAHAMI ELEAZARIS, URALTES CHYMISCHES WERCK (ERFURT, 1735)
British Library

"Although scholars continue to debate whether the work is genuine and question whether Eleazar even existed, the 'Age-Old Chemical Work' nevertheless attempts to show how to make the Philosopher's Stone."

ALEXANDER LOCK
Curator

ALL IS LOST

In this satirical engraving, the seated alchemist uses tongs to grasp a crucible in one hand while with the other he drops a coin (his last?) into another vessel. Behind him, his wife searches for a coin in her empty purse, while their three unruly children scramble in an empty larder above and a fool fans the flames in a brazier. At the right, a heavily robed scholar reads instructions from a manual inscribed *Alghe-Mist*, a pun in Flemish on the word "alchemist", meaning "all is lost." Through the window is a vignette showing the destitute alchemist, his wife, and their three children entering the poorhouse. Philip Galle based this engraving on a 1558 drawing by Pieter Bruegel. In Bruegel's day, alchemy was a recurrent theme in Dutch and Flemish genre painting. The print's Latin inscription is probably an impossible riddle just like the quest for the Philosopher's Stone.

**PHILIP GALLE, AFTER
PIETER BRUEGEL THE ELDER,
THE ALCHEMIST
(ANTWERP, AFTER 1558)**
Metropolitan Museum of Art
▼

▶

AEGIDIUS SADELER II,
HERCULES AND CERBERUS
(1600–1627)
Metropolitan Museum of Art

Clauiger ad fuperos triplici conftricta catena
Tergemini Alcides pertrahit ora canis.

POTIONS AND ALCHEMY

GUARDING THE GATES

In Greek mythology, Cerberus is a monstrous three-headed dog that guards the gates of the Underworld and prevents dead souls from escaping. Cerberus is primarily known for his capture by Hercules. Descending into Hades and capturing the mythical canine is the final and most daunting of Hercules's twelve Labors. In Sadeler's engraving, the strongman Hercules wears his characteristic lion-skin, the prize he garnered from his first Labor, the slaying of the Nemean Lion. Holding a club in one hand and three chains leashing the trio of snarling heads in the other, he drags Cerberus away from the licking flames at the entrance to Hades. After his harrowing of Hell, Hercules delivers the horrific hound to Eurystheus, king of Argos and supervisor of his twelve Labors, after which he returns the monster to the Underworld.

SEEING FLUFFY

In this original drawing by J.K. Rowling, Neville, Ron, Harry, Hermione, and "Gary" (later renamed Dean and cut from this scene) are faced with a terrifying, huge three-headed dog. Each student has a detail appropriate to their character—note Neville's bunny pajamas, Ron's freckles, and Hermione's large front teeth. This early drawing shows us how the characters might have appeared in the author's mind. Originally designed to be part of Chapter Seven, "Draco's Duel," this scene eventually became Chapter Nine and was renamed "The Midnight Duel." Only Hermione has the composure to spot that "Fluffy" is guarding a trapdoor, leading Harry to realize that they have found the hiding place of Hagrid's mysterious package from Gringotts vault 713.

▶

PEN AND INK DRAWING OF HARRY AND HIS FRIENDS BY J.K. ROWLING (1991)
J.K. Rowling

"SEE?" SAID HERMIONE, WHEN HARRY AND RON HAD FINISHED. "THE DOG MUST BE GUARDING FLAMEL'S SORCERER'S STONE! I BET HE ASKED DUMBLEDORE TO KEEP IT SAFE FOR HIM, BECAUSE THEY'RE FRIENDS AND HE KNEW SOMEONE WAS AFTER IT. THAT'S WHY HE WANTED THE STONE MOVED OUT OF GRINGOTTS!"

—*HARRY POTTER AND THE SORCERER'S STONE*

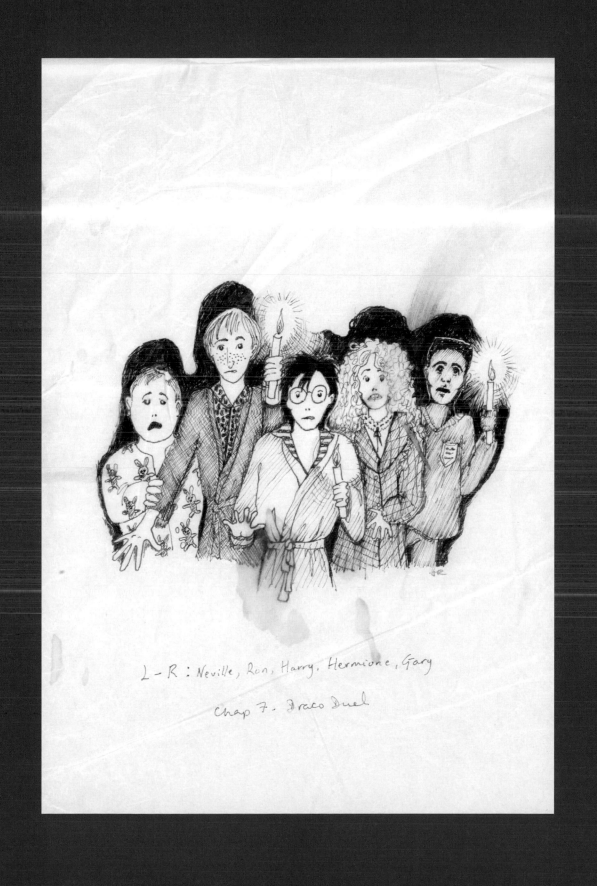

L - R : Neville, Ron, Harry, Hermione, Gary

Chap 7. Draco Duel

THEY WERE LOOKING STRAIGHT INTO THE EYES OF A MONSTROUS DOG, A DOG THAT FILLED THE WHOLE SPACE BETWEEN CEILING AND FLOOR. IT HAD THREE HEADS. THREE PAIRS OF ROLLING, MAD EYES; THREE NOSES, TWITCHING AND QUIVERING IN THEIR DIRECTION; THREE DROOLING MOUTHS, SALIVA HANGING IN SLIPPERY ROPES FROM YELLOWISH FANGS.

—HARRY POTTER AND THE SORCERER'S STONE

QUIRRELL AND THE SORCERER'S STONE

This handwritten draft of "The Man with Two Faces" Chapter Seventeen of *The Sorcerer's Stone*, shows J.K. Rowling's writing in ballpoint pen on unlined paper. While you can see some small deletions in the text, much of the dialogue in this early draft remains the same as the published text. On discovering that Professor Quirrell was behind the attempts to steal the Sorcerer's Stone, not Snape as he had suspected, Harry is given this defiant line: "You haven't got the stone yet [...] Dumbledore will be here soon. He'll stop you." This and Quirrell's next line was cut during the editorial process, in which the confrontation was reorganized. In the published version, Quirrell discloses that he had let the troll into the school immediately after he had bound Harry in ropes.

"J.K. Rowling has expressed how much she loves writing dialogue, and this draft shows how small changes in dialogue can have a powerful effect on characterization."

JOANNA NORLEDGE
Curator

◀

FLUFFY BY JIM KAY
Bloomsbury

▶

A DRAFT OF HARRY POTTER AND THE SORCERER'S STONE, CHAPTER SEVENTEEN, HANDWRITTEN BY J.K. ROWLING
J.K. Rowling

Chapter Seventeen
The Man with Two Faces.

It was Quirrell.

"*You!*" said Harry.

Quirrell smiled, and his face wasn't twitching at all.

"Me," he said calmly.

"But I thought – Snape –"

"Severus?" Quirrell laughed and it wasn't his usual quivering treble either, but cold and sharp. "Yes, Severus does seem the type, doesn't he? So useful to have him swooping around like an overgrown bat. Next to him, who would suspect me? P – p – poor st – st – stuttering P–P– Professor Quirrell."

"But he tried to kill me –"

"No, no, no," said Quirrell. "*I* was trying to kill you. Your friend Miss Granger accidentally knocked me over as she rushed to set fire to Snape. It broke my eye contact with you. Another few seconds and I'd have got you off that broom. I'd have managed it before then if Snape hadn't been muttering a counter-curse, trying to save you."

"He was trying to *save* me?"

"Of course," said Quirrell coolly. "Why do you think he wanted to referee your next match? He was trying to make sure I didn't do it again. Funny, really... he needn't have bothered. I couldn't do anything with Dumbledore watching. All the other teachers thought Snape was trying to stop Gryffindor winning, he did make a fool of himself... ~~and he needn't have bothered~~ and what a waste of time, when ~~in the end~~ after all that, I'm going to kill you ~~now~~ tonight."

Quirrell snapped his fingers. Ropes sprang out of thin air and wrapped themselves tightly around Harry.

"Now, you wait there, Potter, while I examine this interesting mirror –"

It was only then that Harry realised what was standing behind Quirrell. It was the Mirror of Erised.

"You haven't got the stone yet –" said Harry desperately. "Dumbledore will be here soon, he'll stop you –"

"For someone who's about to die, you're very talkative, Potter," said Quirrell, feeling his way around the mirror's frame. "This mirror is the key to finding the stone, it won't take me long – and Dumbledore's in London, I'll be ~~long gone~~ far away by the time he gets here –"

All Harry could think of ~~to do~~ was to keep Quirrell talking.

"~~But~~ That troll at Hallowe'en –"

"Yes, I let it in. I was hoping ~~that~~ some foolhardy student would get themselves killed by it, to give me time to ~~get to~~ the stone. Unfortunately, Snape found out. I think ~~he~~ see that was suspici that ghost with ~~his head hoping off~~ the loose head tipped him off. Snape came straight to the third floor corridor to head me off ... and you didn't get killed by the troll! That was why I tried to finish you at the Quidditch match — but blow me if I didn't fail again."

Quirrell rapped the Mirror of Erised impatiently.

"Dratted thing ... trust Dumbledore to come up with something like this ..." He stared hungrily into the mirror. "I see the stone," he said. "I'm presenting it to my Master ... but where is it?"

He went back to feeling his way around the mirror.

B ~~A sudden~~ ~~ ~~ Harry's mind was racing at his ~~ ~~ ~~ ~~ ~~ moment,"

"What I want more than anything ~~ ~~ ~~ ~~ ~~," he thought, "is to find the stone before Quirrell does. So if I look in the mirror, I should see myself finding it — which means I'll see where it's hidden. But how can I look without him realising what I'm up to? ~~ ~~ I've got to play for time ..."

"I saw you and Snape in the forest," he blurted out.

"Yes," said Quirrell idly, walking around the mirror to look at the back. "He was ~~onto~~ me. Trying to find out how far I'd got. He suspected me all along. Tried to frighten me — as though he could scare me, ~~ ~~ when I had Lord Voldemort ~~ ~~ on my side."

"But Snape always ~~seemed~~ to hate me so much —"

"Oh, he does," Quirrell said casually. "Heavens, yes. He was at ~~school~~ Hogwarts with your father, didn't you know? They loathed each other. But he ~~ ~~ didn't want you ~~dead~~."

"And that warning burned into my bed —"

"Yes, that was me," said Quirrell, now ~~ ~~ feeling the mirror's clawed feet. "I heard you and Weasley in my class, talking about Philosopher's Stones. I ~~ ~~ thought you might try and interfere. ~~ ~~ Pity you didn't heed my ~~warning~~, isn't it? Curiosity has led you to your doom, Potter."

"But I heard you a few days ago, ~~ ~~ sobbing — I thought Snape was ~~threatening~~ you —"

For the first time, a spasm of fear flitted ~~across~~ Quirrell's face.

"Sometimes —" he said, "I find it hard to follow my Master's instructions — he is a great man and I am weak —"

"You mean he was there in the classroom with you?" Harry gasped.

"He is with me wherever I go," said Quirrell softly. "I met ~~ ~~ with him when I travelled round the world, a ~~ ~~ foolish young man, full of ridiculous ideas ~~ ~~ about good and evil. Lord Voldemort showed me how wrong I was. There is no good and evil. There is only power, and those too weak to seek it ... Since then, I have served him faithfully, though I have let him down many times. He has ~~had to be very~~ hard on me." Quirrell shuddered suddenly. "He does not forgive mistakes easily. When I failed to steal the stone from

Dragontea . a'. serpentaria . a'. at
. a'. colubraria ul' inperna a'. auria
nna . a'. uas . a'. luf uocant .

Draco magnus .

CHAPTER **3**

HERBOLOGY

HARRY, RON, AND HERMIONE LEFT THE CASTLE TOGETHER, CROSSED THE VEGETABLE PATCH, AND MADE FOR THE GREENHOUSES, WHERE THE MAGICAL PLANTS WERE KEPT.

—*HARRY POTTER AND THE CHAMBER OF SECRETS*

HERBOLOGY AT HOGWARTS

Herbology classes at Hogwarts took place in the greenhouses on the castle grounds. This is a meticulous drawing by Jim Kay of one of the Herbology greenhouses, showing the structural sections and glass panels. The artist once worked at Kew Gardens in London, where the Palm House, the Temperate House, and the Alpine House proved good sources of inspiration for these drawings. They are excellent examples of specialized greenhouses designed to provide varying environments for plants.

◀

DRAWING OF A HOGWARTS GREENHOUSE BY JIM KAY
Bloomsbury

"The greenhouses in Kay's vision are clearly designed around the plants' needs— some hang, some will creep up walls, some will grow in water, others spread out in the shade."

JOANNA NORLEDGE
Curator

A SQUAT LITTLE WITCH

J.K. Rowling's early drawing of Professor Sprout, made eight years before the publication of *Harry Potter and the Sorcerer's Stone*, shows the character surrounded by the plants studied in her Herbology class. At Hogwarts, Herbology included the study of normal plants as well as magical ones. Are the tendrils spreading from one of the pots actually sneaky Venomous Tentacula, looking for something to chew on? Professor Sprout herself is pictured in her witch's hat, with a spider hanging from its tip, handy for keeping her greenhouses free from plant-eating insects.

▼

PEN AND INK DRAWING OF PROFESSOR POMONA SPROUT BY J.K. ROWLING (DECEMBER 30, 1990)
J.K. Rowling

CULPEPER'S HERBAL

When seeking inspiration for naming her herbs and potions, J.K. Rowling used the herbal of the apothecary Nicholas Culpeper. The book was first published in 1652 as *The English Physician*. It has subsequently appeared in over a hundred editions, and was the first medical book to be published in North America. Culpeper's herbal provides a comprehensive list of native medicinal herbs, indexed against specific illnesses, and prescribes the most effective forms of treatment and when to take them. Culpeper was an unlicensed apothecary, disliked by the medical profession, who jealously guarded their monopoly to practice medicine in London. He came into conflict with the College of Physicians, and in 1642 was apparently tried, but acquitted, for practicing witchcraft.

THREE TIMES A WEEK THEY WENT OUT TO THE GREENHOUSES BEHIND THE CASTLE TO STUDY HERBOLOGY, WITH A DUMPY LITTLE WITCH CALLED PROFESSOR SPROUT, WHERE THEY LEARNED HOW TO TAKE CARE OF ALL THE STRANGE PLANTS AND FUNGI, AND FOUND OUT WHAT THEY WERE USED FOR.

—*HARRY POTTER AND THE SORCERER'S STONE*

"Culpeper was concerned with informing the less educated members of society, and so he wrote in English rather than the traditional Latin."

ALEXANDER LOCK
Curator

▶

CULPEPER'S ENGLISH PHYSICIAN; AND COMPLETE HERBAL (LONDON, 1789)
British Library

CULPEPER's
ENGLISH PHYSICIAN;
AND COMPLETE
HERBAL.

TO WHICH ARE NOW FIRST ADDED,

Upwards of One Hundred additional H E R B S,

WITH A DISPLAY OF THEIR

MEDICINAL AND OCCULT PROPERTIES,

PHYSICALLY APPLIED TO

The CURE of all DISORDERS incident to MANKIND.

TO WHICH ARE ANNEXED,

RULES for Compounding MEDICINE according to the True SYSTEM of NATURE:

FORMING A COMPLETE

FAMILY DISPENSATORY,

And Natural SYSTEM of PHYSIC.

BEAUTIFIED AND ENRICHED WITH

ENGRAVINGS of upwards of Four Hundred and Fifty different PLANTS,

And a SET of ANATOMICAL FIGURES.

ILLUSTRATED WITH NOTES AND OBSERVATIONS,

CRITICAL AND EXPLANATORY.

By E. SIBLY, Fellow of the Harmonic Philosophical Society at PARIS, and
Author of the Complete ILLUSTRATION of ASTROLOGY.

HAPPY THE MAN, WHO STUDYING NATURE'S LAWS,
THROUGH KNOWN EFFECTS CAN TRACE THE SECRET CAUSE.   DRYDEN.

LONDON:
PRINTED FOR THE PROPRIETORS, AND SOLD BY GREEN AND CO. 176, STRAND.
MDCCLXXXIX.

"OH, HELLO THERE!" HE CALLED, BEAMING AROUND AT THE ASSEMBLED STUDENTS. "JUST BEEN SHOWING PROFESSOR SPROUT THE RIGHT WAY TO DOCTOR A WHOMPING WILLOW! BUT I DON'T WANT YOU RUNNING AWAY WITH THE IDEA THAT I'M BETTER AT HERBOLOGY THAN SHE IS! I JUST HAPPEN TO HAVE MET SEVERAL OF THESE EXOTIC PLANTS ON MY TRAVELS . . ."

—PROFESSOR LOCKHART, *HARRY POTTER AND THE CHAMBER OF SECRETS*

MAGICAL GARDENING IMPLEMENTS

Herbology is a mandatory subject taken by all students at Hogwarts, reflecting the importance of plants to magic, medicine, and herbal lore. These gardening implements, made from bone and antler, were used by practitioners of magic specifically for sowing and harvesting plants. It was essential that these tools were formed entirely from natural resources so they did not corrupt the plants being harvested. The materials also had symbolic importance. Tools shaped from antlers, which rise upward above the head, were considered to connect the Earth with the higher spirit world. As antlers are shed and regrown annually, they symbolize the magic of regeneration and renewal.

"Tools like these have been used for thousands of years. Many plants are harvested not only for their medicinal qualities, but for their alleged supernatural powers—in such cases, the rituals involved in gathering them are extremely important."

ALEXANDER LOCK
Curator

◄

GARDENING IMPLEMENTS MADE FROM ANTLER AND BONE
The Museum of Witchcraft and Magic, Boscastle

REMEDY FOR SNAKEBITE

What was one of the most effective remedies for snakebite? This 12th-century manuscript advises the afflicted to seek out two plants known as *Centauria major* and *Centauria minor*. The "greater" and "lesser" centaury were named after the ancient Greek centaur Chiron. In Greek mythology, Chiron was renowned as a physician, astrologer, and oracle. Among his pupils was Asclepius, the god of medicine and healing, who had been rescued as a baby and was taken to Chiron to be reared. In this pen and ink drawing, Chiron is shown handing over the two plants to the toga-wearing Asclepius. A snake can be seen slithering away from under their feet.

▶

**CENTAURY IN AN HERBAL
(ENGLAND, 12TH CENTURY)**
British Library

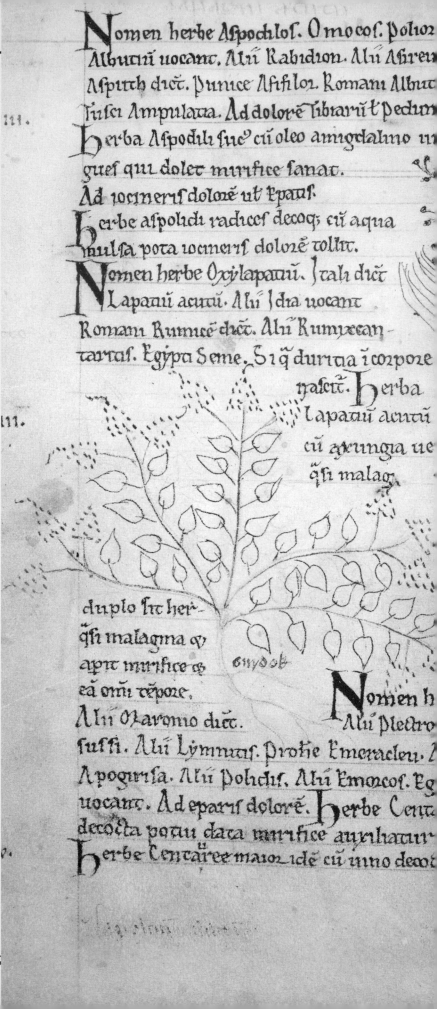

nat nos ipsi experti sumus. Ad uulnia 7 Canceromata. Herba Centaur
maior contrita & apposita. tumorem fieri non patitur. Ad suggillationes &
liuores. Herbe centaurie suci puncti summe facit. Ad uulnia recentia. Her
be centaurie puluis missus plagas conglutinat. ut etiam carnes coerescant
7 centauria maior in aqua decocta. inde uuln̄ foueat̄. Nomen herbe cen
taurea minor. Omoeos. Illebontes. Pphe. Coa
heradeos. Egiptii.
Amaratin Pau. Sir
sozila. Itali. febrifuga.
Alii. fel. t̄re. Romam.
Amaritudo. Has herbas
duas dicun̄ cirocentaurum
iuenisse & eas asclepio dedis
se. unde nom̄ centauria ac
ceperunt. Hasc̄ī locis solidis
& fortibus.

Ad uipere morsum. Herbe Centaurie minore contrita puluis er̄ aut

---

(left margin, upper) Zuburizu. Itali

(left margin, lower) simul contrita facies
nus mirabilit sanat.
paricula q̄ i īgui
e nascit. Herba
lapatiu contusa
ligno i ligno fi ut
ra q̄ axungia facit
n ponis paricula
& recludit. legis
taurea maior.
Punici dic̄t Abus
nas dic̄t. Alii
tinas. Itali fel t̄re
uouis in uino
enis dolorem.
data spleuē ipsa-

DRAGON AND SERPENT

During the Middle Ages, many scholars compiled manuscripts for their own practical use, recording and illustrating the properties of individual plants. This magnificently decorated herbal was made in Lombardy, northern Italy, around the year 1440. It was most probably compiled for a wealthy landowner. Each page has been filled with lifelike drawings of plants and short notes explaining their names. On the right-hand side we can see snakeroot. The author has recorded some of the species' Latin names beside it—"*Dragontea,*" "*serpentaria,*" and "*viperina*" reveal the plant's ability to cure snakebite. A hissing green serpent can also be seen curling around the plant's root. A snarling dragon called in Latin "*Draco magnus*" is perched to its left, painted with a forked tongue and an elaborately knotted tail.

▶

SNAKEROOT IN AN HERBAL (ITALY, 15TH CENTURY)
British Library

"*The term 'snakeroot' is applied today to various plants with medicinal qualities, such as plantain. A poultice of plantain applied to a wound is widely believed to accelerate the healing process.*"

JULIAN HARRISON
Lead Curator

Dolcea. qo. dr. comi. q.
mlti rpicon dicit. sap no.
dicit. nderig ul' eismo a.
mlti uellaseu uera appellit.

Dragontea. a'. serpentaria. a'. asclepias.
a'. colubraria ul' uiperina a'. auricula asi
nina. a'. uuas. a'. lus uocant.

.Draco magnus.

.Dragantu alio noic
algitura. a'. katura a.
sura. dr tragagati.

A CURIOUS HERBAL

A Curious Herbal is a book with a remarkable history. This work was illustrated, engraved, and hand-colored by Elizabeth Blackwell in order to raise funds to have her husband, Alexander, released from a debtors' prison. The book was issued in weekly parts between 1737 and 1739, and contained images of 500 of "the most useful plants, which are now used in the practice of physick." Elizabeth made her drawings at Chelsea Physic Garden in London and then took her drawings to Alexander in prison, where he identified the plants in question. Although the venture raised enough income to secure Alexander's release, he eventually left for Sweden, where he was executed for treason, having become involved in a political conspiracy. Elizabeth died alone in England in 1758.

AND SO THE THREE WITCHES AND THE FORLORN KNIGHT VENTURED FORTH INTO THE ENCHANTED GARDEN, WHERE RARE HERBS, FRUIT, AND FLOWERS GREW IN ABUNDANCE ON EITHER SIDE OF THE SUNLIT PATHS.

—*THE TALES OF BEEDLE THE BARD*

▲ DRACONTIUM, IN ELIZABETH BLACKWELL, *A CURIOUS HERBAL, CONTAINING FIVE HUNDRED CUTS OF THE MOST USEFUL PLANTS WHICH ARE NOW USED IN THE PRACTICE OF PHYSICK*, 2 VOLS (LONDON, 1737–9)
British Library

GERARD'S HERBAL

John Gerard was an English herbalist, whose most famous work was entitled *The Herball or Generall Historie of Plantes*. Gerard maintained his own garden in Holborn, London. He cultivated all manner of plants there, including exotic specimens such as the recently discovered potato. *The Herball* contains more than 1,800 woodcut illustrations. Only sixteen of these were actually original to Gerard's work, the remainder having been taken (without ɑɔknowledgement) from a book printed in Germany ɑ few years previously. The final woodcut in the book illustrates "the tree bearing geese"—a tree that supposedly grew goose embryos inside its fruit. Gerard claimed to have seen one of these in Lancashire, England.

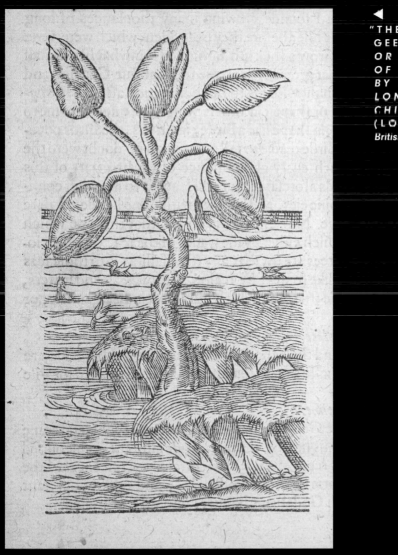

◄ "THE TREE BEARING GEESE," IN *THE HERBALL OR GENERALL HISTORIE OF PLANTES. GATHERED BY JOHN GERARDE OF LONDON, MASTER IN CHIRURGERIE* (LONDON, 1597)
British Library

HIS HEART SANK. HE HAD NOT ADDED SYRUP OF HELLEBORE, BUT HAD PROCEEDED STRAIGHT TO THE FOURTH LINE OF THE INSTRUCTIONS AFTER ALLOWING HIS POTION TO SIMMER FOR SEVEN MINUTES.

—HARRY POTTER AND THE ORDER OF THE PHOENIX

DRIED GARDENS

For hundreds of years, apothecaries, professors, and ardent students of botany have diligently pressed and preserved plants in so-called "dried gardens" or *horti sicci*. This practice allowed for the plants to be studied and researched regardless of the change of seasons or garden accessibility. Around the turn of the 18th century—with new plant classification systems shaking scientific circles—loose-leaf pages became the preferred method of preserving plants and recording their data, and allowed for rearrangement and easy comparison. The pressed plant on this page seems to be *Adonis vernalis*, or fake hellebore. Though the plant contains toxic substances, the aboveground parts of the plant have been used in folk medicinal remedies for fever and intestinal worms. In the magical world of Harry Potter, hellebore is a primary ingredient in the Draught of Peace.

▲
ADONIS HELLEBORE, IN *CATALOGUS PLANTARUM FLORE* (POSSIBLY PORTUGAL, 18TH CENTURY)
The LuEsther T. Mertz Library of the New York Botanical Garden

Crocus Vernus aureus variegatus.

Helleborus niger flore viride.

Crocus Vernus polyanthos flore luteo.

THE GARDEN OF EICHSTÄTT

Commissioned in 1611 by Johann Konrad von Gemmingen, Prince Bishop of Eichstätt in Bavaria, the *Hortus Eystettensis* is a magnificent catalog of the plants grown in the bishop's palace garden. The book was produced by Basilius Besler, a botanist from Nuremberg, who supervised both the garden and the artists who drew the plants. This book was a major undertaking, with the flowers having to be illustrated as they bloomed throughout the seasons. It contains 367 engravings and was printed on the largest paper then available. Harry Potter may have forgotten the hellebore in his Draught of Peace, but it was well known to Besler, who cultivated several varieties of the plant in the garden. One, *Helleborus niger* (black hellebore), had been used as a medicine since antiquity, although today it is considered a poison.

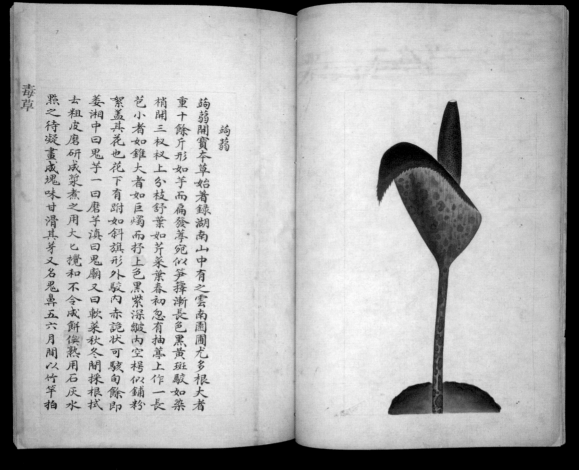

▲
DEVIL'S TONGUE, IN
***DU CAO* (CHINA, 19TH**
CENTURY)
British Library

DEVIL'S TONGUE

This beautifully illustrated Chinese manuscript deals with the topic of poisonous and medicinal plants. The picture shows a lily with an elegant, single bloom called devil's tongue, also known as "konjac," "voodoo lily," or "snake palm." Today, devil's tongue is used in making weight-loss supplements and facial massage products. The exotic-looking flower is a member of the same genus as titan arum, the worst-smelling plant on Earth.

"Herbal medicine has a long history in China. According to tradition, it originated with the mythical emperor, Shen Nong (the 'Divine Farmer'), who is believed to have been the inventor of agriculture and medicine, as well as the author of the first book on the subject, the Bencaojing."

EMMA GOODLIFFE
Curator

THE TEMPLE OF FLORA

Described as a "visually magnificent failure," this elaborate book on botany nearly bankrupted its author, the physician and botanist, Robert John Thornton. Using a range of modern printing techniques, Thornton employed teams of master engravers and colorists to reproduce highly dramatized paintings of flora from across the world. Thornton's timing was unfortunate, however: War with France brought higher taxes and meant that the target audience (the wealthy) had less disposable income for such an expensive book. Despite being granted a license from Parliament to hold a fund-raising lottery, Thornton never recovered his investment.

"CAREFUL, WEASLEY, CAREFUL!" CRIED PROFESSOR SPROUT AS THE BEANS BURST INTO BLOOM BEFORE THEIR VERY EYES.

—*HARRY POTTER AND THE PRISONER OF AZKABAN*

*"This exquisite black flower is called 'dragon arum' (*Dracunculus vulgaris*), also known by the somewhat less appealing name 'stink lily.' It produces the smell of putrefying meat to attract flies for pollination."*

ALEXANDER LOCK
Curator

A MANDRAKE ROOT

Harry and his friends first came face-to-face with a mandrake in Greenhouse Three, which contained the most "interesting and dangerous plants" at Hogwarts. As Hermione Granger immediately knew, "Mandrake, or Mandragora, is a powerful restorative [...] used to return people who have been transfigured or cursed, to their original state [...] The cry of the Mandrake is fatal to anyone who hears it." While the mandrakes encountered by Harry, Hermione, and Ron are still young, this specimen has the appearance of a bearded old man. The resemblance of mandrakes to the human form has influenced many cultures over the centuries. In reality, the mandrake's root and leaves are poisonous, and it can induce hallucinations.

◀

**A MANDRAKE ROOT
(ENGLAND, 16TH OR
17TH CENTURY)**
Science Museum

"AS OUR MANDRAKES ARE ONLY SEEDLINGS, THEIR CRIES WON'T KILL YET," SHE SAID CALMLY, AS THOUGH SHE'D JUST DONE NOTHING MORE EXCITING THAN WATER A BEGONIA.

—PROFESSOR SPROUT, *HARRY POTTER AND THE CHAMBER OF SECRETS*

HARVESTING A MANDRAKE

According to medieval herbals, mandrakes were said to cure headaches, earache, gout, and insanity, among other ailments. Harvesting them, however, has long been deemed an extremely hazardous business. The best way to obtain the plant safely was to unearth its roots with an ivory stake, attaching one end of a cord to the mandrake and the other to a dog. The dog could be encouraged to move forward by blowing a horn, dragging the mandrake with it. The sound of the horn would also serve to drown out the plant's terrible shriek.

"A macabre feature of the mandrake in the foreground of this image is the two severed hands growing out of its stems. These symbolize the plant's use as an anesthetic during amputations."

JULIAN HARRISON
Lead Curator

▲
GIOVANNI CADAMOSTO'S ILLUSTRATED HERBAL (ITALY OR GERMANY, 15TH CENTURY)
British Library

THE MALE AND FEMALE

MANDRAKE

This illuminated manuscript contains an Arabic version of Books Three and Four of *De materia medica* ("On medical material"), originally written in Greek by Pedanius Dioscorides. Dioscorides was a botanist and pharmacologist, working as a physician in the Roman army. The manuscript contains no fewer than 287 color illustrations of plants, together with spaces left blank for a further 52 drawings. Dioscorides was one of the first authors to distinguish between the male and female mandrake, as shown here. One should almost refer to them as the "mandrake" and "womandrake." However, this identification is miseIading; Dioscorides had actually identified two different species of mandrake native to the Mediterranean.

▲
THE MALE AND FEMALE
MANDRAKE, IN *KITĀB
MAWĀDD AL-'ILĀJ*
(BAGHDAD, 14TH CENTURY)
British Library

"This illustration appears to be drawn from life—Jim Kay was previously a curator at the Royal Botanic Gardens, Kew—and it references the natural studies of plants that are typically found in any botanical library."

JOANNA NORLEDGE
Curator

▲
**STUDY OF MANDRAKES
BY JIM KAY**
Bloomsbury

INSTEAD OF ROOTS, A SMALL, MUDDY, AND EXTREMELY UGLY BABY POPPED OUT OF THE EARTH. THE LEAVES WERE GROWING RIGHT OUT OF HIS HEAD. HE HAD PALE GREEN, MOTTLED SKIN, AND WAS CLEARLY BAWLING AT THE TOP OF HIS LUNGS.

—HARRY POTTER AND THE CHAMBER OF SECRETS

Gnomen-Figuren des Gartentechnischen Geschäfts von Ludwig Möller in Erfurt.

▲
GNOMES, IN KARL GOTZE,
*ALBUM FÜR TEPPICHGÄRTNEREI
UND GRUPPENBEPFLANZUNG*
(ERFURT, 1897)
*The LuEsther T. Mertz Library of the
New York Botanical Garden*

GNOMES GALORE

While de-gnoming may have been a chore for the Weasleys, gnoming—or beautifying gardens with gnome sculptures—has been a popular hobby for families since the 1870s when August Heissner and Philipp Griebel began mass-producing garden gnomes in their workshops in Gräfenroda, Germany. This 1897 catalog of the Ludwig Möller Garden Company illustrates a selection of gnomes designed for garden beds and shrubberies near outdoor seating areas. Unlike the gnomes resembling "fat little Father Christmases" that Ron notes are all the rage among Muggles, the Thuringian retailers emphasize that "care has been taken to avoid unattractive or even ugly facial expressions so that these figures could not fail to achieve one of their most important purposes: delighting children."

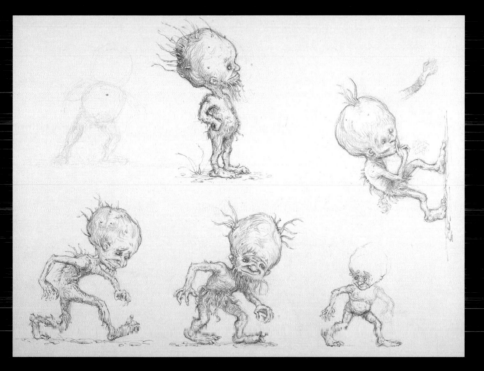

◀

**STUDY OF
GNOMES
BY JIM KAY**
Bloomsbury

IT WAS SMALL AND LEATHERY LOOKING, WITH A LARGE, KNOBBY, BALD HEAD EXACTLY LIKE A POTATO. RON HELD IT AT ARM'S LENGTH AS IT KICKED OUT AT HIM WITH ITS HORNY LITTLE FEET . . .
—*HARRY POTTER AND THE CHAMBER OF SECRETS*

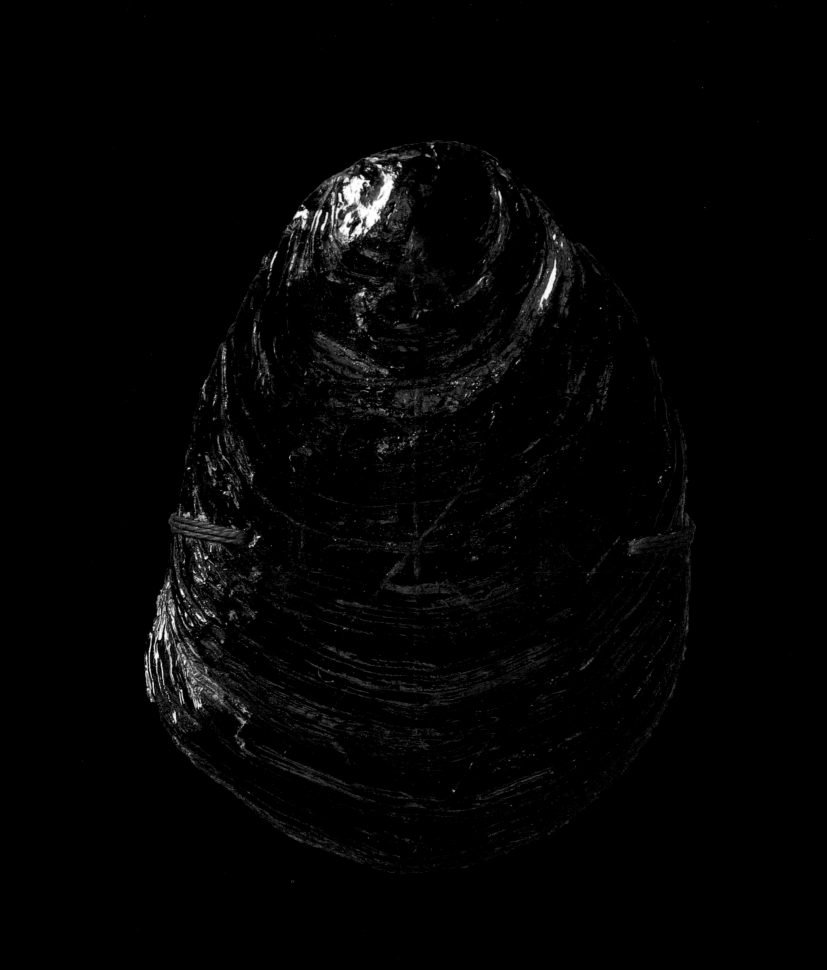

CHAPTER 4

CHARMS

DRAWING OF
THE OPENING TO
DIAGON ALLEY BY
J.K. ROWLING (1990)
J.K. Rowling

INTO THE ALLEY

This drawing reveals, in six stages, how the entrance arch to Diagon Alley appears when tapped three times by Hagrid's umbrella at the beginning of *The Sorcerer's Stone*. This fully worked-out visualization shows how J.K. Rowling rooted the magic in the book as closely as possible to real-world logic. The concept of bricks reorganizing themselves into an archway is far more plausible than an opening simply appearing out of the blue. These imaginative touches, and the serious considerations that have gone in to explaining magical processes, underline what makes J.K. Rowling's world so vivid and real to so many readers.

THE BRICK HE HAD TOUCHED QUIVERED—IT WRIGGLED—IN THE MIDDLE, A SMALL HOLE APPEARED—IT GREW WIDER AND WIDER—A SECOND LATER THEY WERE FACING AN ARCHWAY LARGE ENOUGH EVEN FOR HAGRID, AN ARCHWAY ONTO A COBBLED STREET THAT TWISTED AND TURNED OUT OF SIGHT.

—*HARRY POTTER AND THE SORCERER'S STONE*

DIAGON ALLEY BY
MARY GRANDPRÉ

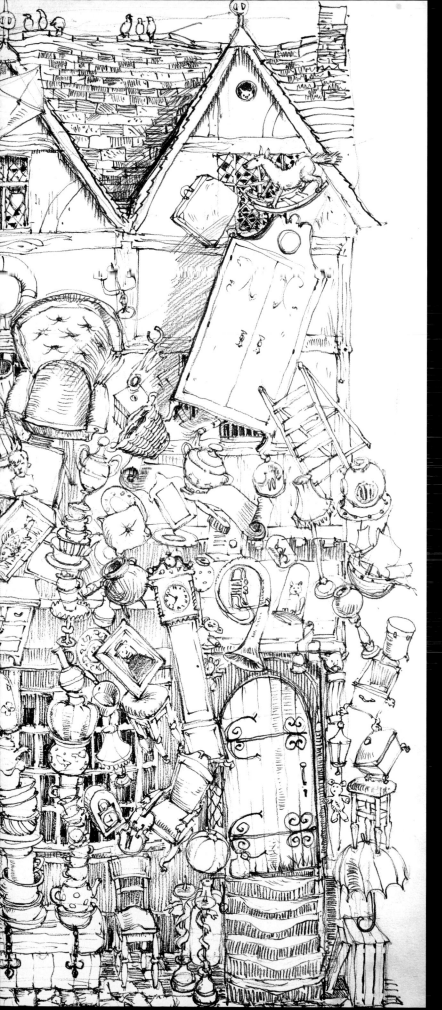

A TRIP TO THE SHOPS

Jim Kay created fantastically meticulous drawings showing the panorama of the shops along Diagon Alley. The atmosphere of this renowned street is captured in the uneven cobbles and the fountainhead beneath the street sign. The shop in the foreground of the drawing at left has hung a vast array of wares all over the building. Why limit yourself to a window display when magic can adorn the whole shop front? Kay chose clever, fun, and personal names for the shops. "Twinkles Telescopes," for example, was inspired by a theatrical store from his childhood called Sally Twinkles. The nut store, "Tut's Nuts," was named after the seeds taken from Tutankhamun's tomb and stored in Kew Gardens, where the artist once worked.

◄

DRAWING OF DIAGON ALLEY BY JIM KAY
Bloomsbury

DECIDING ON A SORTING HAT

▶
NOTES ON SORTING THE
STUDENTS BY J.K. ROWLING
J.K. Rowling

J.K. Rowling spent five years planning out Harry Potter's world and his story. She decided that Hogwarts would have four school houses—Gryffindor, Ravenclaw, Hufflepuff, and Slytherin—with distinct qualities attributed to each. After that, she had to work out how the students would be sorted into the houses. These notes show the author listing some possible ways. The note "statues" represents her idea that four statues of the founders in the Entrance Hall might come alive and select students from the group in front of them (an idea Rowling later modified for the Sorting Ceremony at the North American school of magic, Ilvermorny, as she wrote on Pottermore). Other ideas included a ghost court, a riddle, or prefects choosing students. The Sorting Hat is also shown here, complete with rips, patches, and a grinning mouth.

"FINALLY, I WROTE A LIST OF THE WAYS IN WHICH PEOPLE CAN BE CHOSEN: EENY MEENY MINY MO, SHORT STRAWS, CHOSEN BY TEAM CAPTAINS, NAMES OUT OF A HAT—NAMES OUT OF A TALKING HAT— PUTTING ON A HAT—THE SORTING HAT."
—J.K. ROWLING ON POTTERMORE

(Ghost) Court   N

Hat

Arbitrary List   M

Gateway   M

Statues   N

Selection Committee MN
(Prefects / Hs of H etc)

Question or Riddle M

Forget Song,
~~Just~~ put on Hat.

Dumbledore
|
Forest
Quidditch Trials
Corridor

Snape

Does Scar
have to happen
at feast

Oh I might not be ~~that~~ ~~look too~~ pretty
But don't judge on what you see
I'll eat myself if you can find
A smarter hat than me

Dumbledore & Snape

Peeves

Gobi 2

THE SORTING

HAT SONG

At the start of every academic year at Hogwarts, new students are sorted in to their houses by the Sorting Hat. This is J.K. Rowling's original, handwritten draft of the song that the hat sings at Harry's Sorting Ceremony in his first year. The draft contains some crossings-out and additional edits, but most of these lines survived in the final published text of *The Sorcerer's Stone*.

▶
**THE SORTING
HAT SONG
BY J.K. ROWLING**
J.K. Rowling

◀
**THE SORTING HAT
BY MARY GRANDPRÉ**
Scholastic

Oh, you may not think I'm pretty
But don't judge on what you see
I'll eat myself if you can find
A smarter hat than me
You can keep your bowlers black
Your top hats sleek and tall
For I'm the Hogwarts Sorting Hat
And I can cap them all
~~There can tell you the~~
There's nothing hidden in your ~~head~~ head
The Sorting Hat can't see
So try me on and I will tell you
Where you ought to be.

You might belong in Gryffindor
Where dwell the brave at heart
~~It's daring, nerve and chivalry~~
Or Huff- If you have ~~their~~
~~Eat~~ Their daring, nerve and chivalry
Set Gryffindors apart
You ~~could be born for~~ might belong in Hufflepuff
~~who~~ Where ~~all~~ they are ~~for~~ just and loyal
~~That patient~~ The patient Hufflepuffs are true
And unafraid of toil
~~You may~~ Or Ravenclaw could be your house
~~The house for~~

You ~~might belong~~ in Ravenclaw
Where ~~those~~ all quick wits are found
The ~~straight~~ wisest and most learned minds

If you've a ready mind
For those of wit and learning
For Ravenclaw's kind
Are...

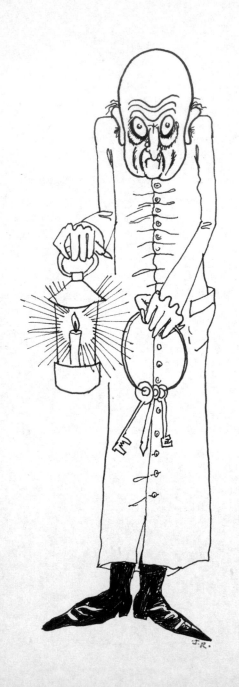

ARGUS FILCH

Argus Filch, the caretaker at Hogwarts, often came close to discovering Harry Potter on his nighttime adventures around the school. Harry only escaped detection thanks to his Invisibility Cloak, which once belonged to his father, James Potter. The lamp held by Filch while he was patrolling the school corridors, shown here in a sketch by J.K. Rowling, enabled him to spot any students wandering the castle when they should have been tucked up in bed. This drawing shows Filch with several worry lines on his forehead, perhaps caused by years of chasing after misbehaving pupils. "Argus" or "Argos" is a name from Greek mythology for a many-eyed or one-hundred-eyed giant whose epithet, "Panoptes," means "all-seeing."

◀

**SKETCH OF ARGUS FILCH
BY J.K. ROWLING (1990)**
J.K. Rowling

**"HOW EXPERIMENTS TO BE INVISIBLE
MUST BE PREPARED," IN *THE BOOK OF
KING SOLOMON CALLED THE KEY OF
KNOWLEDGE* (ENGLAND, 17TH CENTURY)**
British Library
▼

MAKE ME TO BE INVYSIBLE

For those who won't inherit an Invisibility Cloak, other methods of disappearing must be found instead. *The Key of Knowledge* was an instructional text on magic that was spuriously attributed to King Solomon. Here it cites a charm to achieve invisibility. The method proposed varies from manuscript to manuscript, because the book was widely shared, copied, and recopied by students of magic. This manuscript once belonged to the English poet Gabriel Harvey. Care should be taken when reciting this spell, however—*The Key of Knowledge* does not include a charm to make yourself reappear again!

OLGA HUNT'S BROOMSTICK

Few charmed objects are more closely associated with the Western image of the witch than the broomstick. Although the tradition has ancient roots in pagan fertility rights, the connection between witchcraft and broomsticks developed significantly in the art and popular superstitions that fed the witch hysteria of 16th- and 17th-century Europe. This colorful broomstick was once owned by a Devonshire woman named Olga Hunt. When there was a full moon, Olga could be spotted with her broomstick leaping around Haytor Rocks on Dartmoor, much to the alarm of courting couples and campers!

AS EVERY SCHOOL-AGE WIZARD KNOWS,
THE FACT THAT WE FLY ON BROOMSTICKS
IS PROBABLY OUR WORST-KEPT SECRET.
NO MUGGLE ILLUSTRATION OF A WITCH
IS COMPLETE WITHOUT A BROOM [...]
BROOMSTICKS AND MAGIC ARE INEXTRICABLY
LINKED IN THE MUGGLE MIND.
—*QUIDDITCH THROUGH THE AGES*

▶
**BROOMSTICK BELONGING
TO OLGA HUNT (ENGLAND,
20TH CENTURY)**
*The Museum of Witchcraft and
Magic, Boscastle*

A CLOUD OF KEYS

These two draft sketches show how Jim Kay created some of his
illustrations, using a detailed pencil sketch that was then digitally
colored in or overlaid with a watercolor painting. Here you can see him
experimenting with the design and colors of the winged keys, capturing
the "whirl of rainbow feathers" described in *The Sorcerer's Stone*. The keys
have been charmed by Professor Filius Flitwick as one of the protections
put in place by the Hogwarts teachers to guard the Sorcerer's Stone.
Harry used his broomstick-flying skills to capture the one that would open
a magically protected locked door.

▼ ▶
STUDIES OF WINGED
KEYS BY JIM KAY
Bloomsbury

HARRY AND DRACO

The world of magic was new and complicated for Harry when he arrived at Hogwarts, but in his very first flying lesson, having never previously touched a broom, he flew so naturally that Professor McGonagall instantly whisked him away to meet the Gryffindor Quidditch team captain. Harry became the youngest Seeker in a century to play in a Hogwarts Quidditch game. In this painting by Jim Kay, Harry is shown with his cape billowing and his hands firmly clasped around his broomstick, while a rain-blurred Draco Malfoy heads toward him in the background.

WITH A ROAR FROM THE CROWD TO SPEED THEM UPWARD, THE FOURTEEN PLAYERS ROSE TOWARD THE LEADEN SKY. HARRY FLEW HIGHER THAN ANY OF THEM, SQUINTING AROUND FOR THE SNITCH.

—*HARRY POTTER AND THE CHAMBER OF SECRETS*

"Kay's painting brings to life the opening Quidditch match against the Slytherin team in Harry's second year. In the match, a Bludger went rogue and followed Harry relentlessly, eventually breaking his arm. Despite this, Harry caught the Snitch and won the game."

JOANNA NORLEDGE
Curator

▶

HARRY POTTER AND DRACO MALFOY PLAYING QUIDDITCH BY JIM KAY
Bloomsbury

A WITCH AND HER FAMILIAR

In 1621, Anne Fairfax, the younger daughter of Edward Fairfax of Fewston, Yorkshire, died suddenly. Two of her sisters, together with a friend, accused some local women of practicing witchcraft. The women were taken to trial, but the case collapsed when the friend confessed that the whole thing had been a hoax. Edward Fairfax, however, remained resolute in his belief that Anne's death was caused by witches. This manuscript sets out his case for the prosecution. A later illustrator has added drawings of the "witches" and their familiars—demons or spirits, often in the form of an animal, that accompany and obey witches. One witch, "Margaret Wait the elder" is described as a widow whose "husband died by the hand of the executioner. Her familiar is a deformed thing with many feet, rough with hair, the bigness of a cat, and the name of it is unknown."

▲
A DISCOURSE OF WITCHCRAFT AS IT WAS ACTED IN THE FAMILY OF MR. EDWARD FAIRFAX OF FUYSTONE (ENGLAND, 18TH CENTURY)
British Library

THE LANCASHIRE WITCHES

As the anonymous author of this book noted, the English county of Lancashire is "famous for witches and the very strange pranks they have played." Lancashire's popular association with witchery stems from the famous Pendle trials of 1612, when some nineteen people were accused of practicing witchcraft. While the story of the Pendle witch craze is an unhappy one—the majority of the accused were hanged—the author of this text was eager to portray Lancashire witches in a more positive light. The book is illustrated with simple woodcuts, including this picture of a jolly witch mounting a broomstick.

"The text accompanying this illustration states, 'Lancashire witches chiefly divert themselves in merriment and sport.' Perhaps it is little wonder, then, that Quidditch Through the Ages *cites the first known account of a Quidditch match in 1385, as 'a game in Lancashire.'"*

ALEXANDER LOCK
Curator

▼
*THE HISTORY OF THE
LANCASHIRE WITCHES
(COVENTRY, 1825)*
British Library

22

in destroying and laming of cattle, and drowning ships at sea, by raising storms. But it appears that the Lancashire witches chiefly divert themselves in merriment and sport; therefore they are found to be more sociable than any others.

CHAP. XI.
A short description of the famous Lapland Witches.

WITCHCRAFT ON TRIAL

Like the Pendle witch trials in Lancashire, England, in 1612, the Salem witch crisis eighty years later depended largely on local feuds, religious strife, and long-held cultural beliefs about women and gender. In Puritan New England, many leaders used accusations of witchcraft as a way to control "disruptive" female behavior. Cotton Mather, a Congregational minister in Boston and staunch defender of Puritan orthodoxy, wrote *The Wonders of the Invisible World: Being an Account of the Tryals of Several Witches, Lately Executed in New-England* in 1693 as his justification for the Salem witchcraft crisis and executions. While Mather attacked witches as the embodiment of evil and defended the court's verdicts, he also voiced his great discomfort with the court's admission of spectral evidence (testimony from dreams, ghosts, and visions). Mather called on the court to admit only testimony from human witnesses, rather than spectral testimony, in the persecution of witches. Only humans, he argued, should "turn the scale" of justice in court.

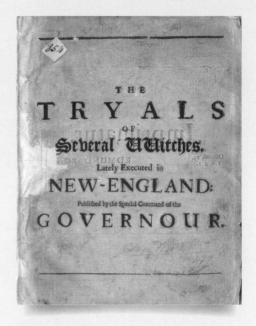

▲

COTTON MATHER, *THE WONDERS OF THE INVISIBLE WORLD* (LONDON, 1693)
New-York Historical Society

A MAGICAL RING

This 4th-century papyrus is part of an ancient Greek handbook for magic. As well as containing charms to discover thieves and to reveal the secret thoughts of men, the handbook describes how to prepare a magical ring. The owner was advised to inscribe the ring with a charm, according to the following formula: "May something never happen as long as this remains buried." It was intended that the ring be hidden in the ground, in order to prevent something from happening. By inscribing and burying the ring, the owner could specify, for example, that they did not want a rival to be lucky in love. With the exception of one added word, the inscription reads the same in either direction. This is a well-known characteristic of magical charms.

ABRACADABRA

The "Abracadabra" spell has been used by generations of magicians to conjure rabbits out of hats. In ancient times, however, the same word was held to be a charm with healing powers. Its first documented use appears in the *Liber Medicinalis* or "Book of Medicine" written by Quintus Serenus Sammonicus in the 2nd century C.E. Serenus was a physician to the Emperor Caracalla, prescribing the charm "Abracadabra" as a cure for malaria. Sufferers were instructed to write out the word again and again, leaving out one letter each time. This would produce a "cone-shaped" text. The charm was then worn as an amulet around the neck in order to drive out the fever.

"The Abracadabra text is outlined in red ink in the margin of this manuscript. Serenus further recommended that flax, the fat of the lion, or coral stones could be used to fix the charm around one's neck."

JULIAN HARRISON
Lead Curator

▶
LIBER MEDICINALIS (CANTERBURY, 13TH CENTURY)
British Library

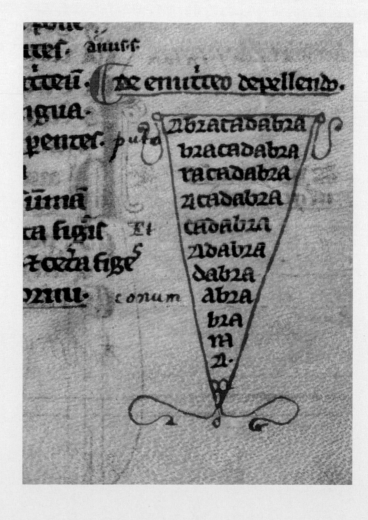

◀
A RING CAPTIONED "MAY SOMETHING NEVER HAPPEN AS LONG AS THIS REMAINS BURIED," IN A GREEK HANDBOOK FOR MAGIC (THEBES, 4TH CENTURY)
British Library

HOW TO TURN YOURSELF INTO A LION

In Ethiopia, magical practitioners commonly make collections of charms, spells, and the names of plants and their properties, which are then copied into handbooks like this one. This page has been removed from a magical recipe book. It contains charms for reversing spells and for binding demons. One charm in particular supplies the formula for changing yourself into a lion or another beast: "With red ink, write these secret names on a piece of white silk. To transform yourself into a lion, tie the silk to your head; to become a python, tie it on your arm; to turn into an eagle, tie it on your shoulder."

"TRANSFIGURATION IS SOME OF THE MOST COMPLEX AND DANGEROUS MAGIC YOU WILL LEARN AT HOGWARTS," SHE SAID. "ANYONE MESSING AROUND IN MY CLASS WILL LEAVE AND NOT COME BACK. YOU HAVE BEEN WARNED."

—PROFESSOR McGONAGALL,
HARRY POTTER AND THE SORCERER'S STONE

▲
A CHARM TO TURN SOMEONE INTO A LION, A PYTHON, OR AN EAGLE (ETHIOPIA, 18TH CENTURY)
British Library

A LOVE CHARM

Love potions and charms are still widely used across the world. Sometimes this type of magic even appeared at Hogwarts— from Professor Slughorn brewing Amortentia in class to Ron Weasley accidentally ingesting Romilda Vane's love potion. Made in the Netherlands, the love charm shown here is rich in symbolism that imbued the object with magical power. Painted onto an oyster shell to ensure fertility, the charm was produced for a couple whose first initials were J and R. Red thread binds the letters together while a pair of touching hearts represent their love. Above these letters are the couple's star signs—♉ for Taurus and ♊ for Gemini.

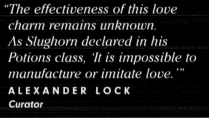

▶
LOVE CHARM (NETHERLANDS, 20TH CENTURY)
The Museum of Witchcraft and Magic, Boscastle

"The effectiveness of this love charm remains unknown. As Slughorn declared in his Potions class, 'It is impossible to manufacture or imitate love.'"
ALEXANDER LOCK
Curator

"PROFESSOR, I'M REALLY SORRY TO DISTURB YOU," SAID HARRY AS QUIETLY AS POSSIBLE, WHILE RON STOOD ON TIPTOE, ATTEMPTING TO SEE PAST SLUGHORN INTO HIS ROOM, "BUT MY FRIEND RON'S SWALLOWED A LOVE POTION BY MISTAKE. YOU COULDN'T MAKE HIM AN ANTIDOTE, COULD YOU?"
—HARRY POTTER AND THE HALF-BLOOD PRINCE

Of The Constellations

ANother Company of Stars that encompass the pole of ye Eclip: & lie dispersed in various places, the antients formed an Image or Constellation called ye Dragon (see fig 3) wreathing & twisting it Self betwixt the two bears, it is a noble Constellation, having Stars in every one of ye 12 Signs & the pole of ye Eliptick is in the very middle of it, (at p) it hath one Star of ye Second Magnitude, (at s) being ye last but two in ye tail, the Star (at o) is called Rasaben, being a bright Star in the head of ye Dragon, famous for that ye Ingenious

Draco the Dragon Fig. 3.

Mr Robert Hook fellow of ye Royal Society, made use of this Star, to attempt the Proof of the Motion of ye Earth by observation, in 1674 where he observed (as ye Reverend mr Flamsteed hath divers times since) a parallax of the Earths Annual orb which infallibly proves the Motion of the Earth to be true, according to ye Doctrine of Copernicus,

Behind the neck of the Dragon, the antients formed another Constellation of Stars into ye Image of a Swan (see fig 4) the Star near the Tail (at m) is of ye 2 Magnitude, & is called Arideof or Arided; & near the Star in its breast, where ye letter (n) is placed; a New Star appeared in the year 1601, & after some time dis appeared, in the year 1658 it appeared again, & likewise in the year

Cygnus the Swan Fig. 4.

CHAPTER **5**

ASTRONOMY

LISTS OF HOGWARTS SUBJECTS AND TEACHERS

In this handwritten note, which was made as she was writing *The Sorcerer's Stone*, J.K. Rowling has listed the subjects taught at Hogwarts alongside the prospective names of their teachers. Here you get a glimpse of some of the revisions and choices J.K. Rowling made as she developed Harry Potter's wizarding world. An early moniker for the Professor of Astronomy is recorded here as "Aurelia Sinistra." This later developed into "Aurora Sinistra." J.K. Rowling often uses Latin words for her names and spells. "Aurora," which means "the dawn," can also refer to the natural phenomenon that occurs near the magnetic poles, creating breathtaking light displays in the sky. As well as meaning "left-hand side," "Sinistra" is also the name of a star in the constellation of Ophiuchus, better known as the Serpent Bearer.

"The lists of Defense Against the Dark Arts teachers include unused characters with unfamiliar names like Enid Pettigrew, Oakden Hernshaw, and Mylor Silvanus, none of whom appear in the published books."

JOANNA NORLEDGE
Curator

◀ ▶
LISTS OF HOGWARTS SUBJECTS AND TEACHERS BY J.K. ROWLING
J.K. Rowling

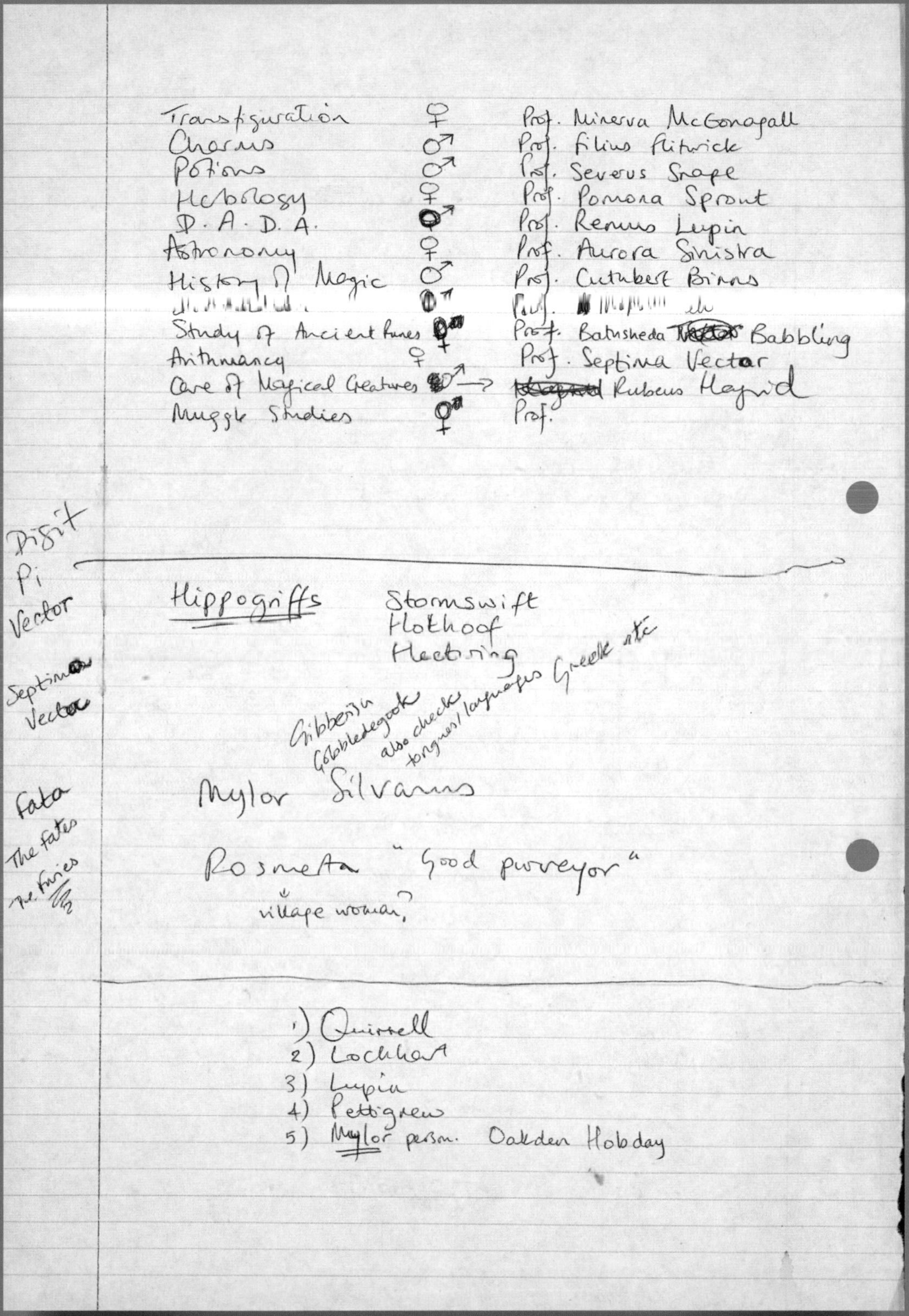

Transfiguration ♀ Prof. Minerva McGonagall
Charms ♀♂ Prof. Filius Flitwick
Potions ♀♂ Prof. Severus Snape
Herbology ♀ Prof. Pomona Sprout
D.A.D.A. ♀♂ Prof. Remus Lupin
Astronomy ♀♂ Prof. Aurora Sinistra
History of Magic ♂♀ Prof. Cuthbert Binns
~~·········~~ ~~·········~~
Study of Ancient Runes ♀♂ Prof. Bathsheda ~~Vector~~ Babbling
Arithmancy ♀♂ Prof. Septima Vector
Care of Magical Creatures ♀♂→ ~~Hagrid~~ Rubeus Hagrid
Muggle Studies ♀♂ Prof.

Digit
Pi
Vector

Septima
Vector

Fata
The Fates
re. Furies

Hippogriffs   Stormswift
                    Flothoof
                    Fleetwing

Gibberish
Gobbledegook
also check tongues/languages Greek etc

Mylor Silvanus

Rosmeta "Good purveyor"
         village woman?

1) Quirrell
2) Lockhart
3) Lupin
4) Pettigrew
5) ~~Mylor~~ persn. Oakden Hobday

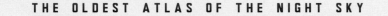

THE OLDEST ATLAS OF THE NIGHT SKY

In 1907, a Hungarian-British archaeologist named Aurel Stein was searching for artifacts in the desert on the southern Silk Road. He entered a cave in Dunhuang, Central China, that had been sealed for thousands of years and stumbled upon an amazing discovery—the cave was a treasure trove containing 40,000 ancient Buddhist manuscripts, paintings, and documents. This paper scroll was among them, the oldest preserved star atlas from any civilization. At the time that the atlas was made, it was believed that the movement of the stars reflected the actions of the emperor and his court on Earth. A solar eclipse, for example, might be interpreted as a sign of a forthcoming coup. The scroll shows more than 1,300 stars visible to the naked eye in the Northern Hemisphere. It is staggering to think that a chart of such accuracy was created by observation alone—the Dunhuang Star Atlas is the oldest map of the night sky, yet it stands up well compared to modern charts today.

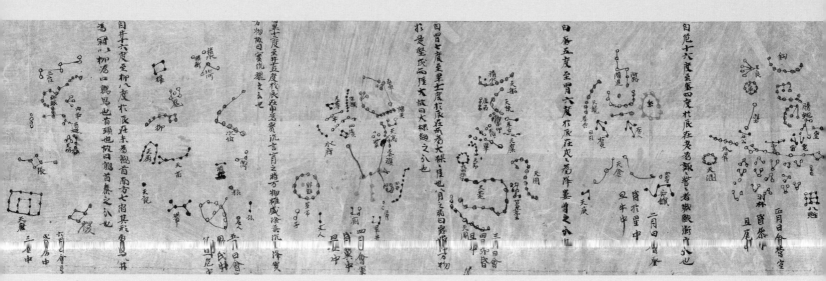

"LIE BACK UPON THE FLOOR," SAID FIRENZE IN HIS CALM VOICE, "AND OBSERVE THE HEAVENS. HERE IS WRITTEN, FOR THOSE WHO CAN SEE, THE FORTUNE OF OUR RACES."

—HARRY POTTER AND THE ORDER OF THE PHOENIX

"This star atlas is a remarkable survival. It is astonishing to think that it was created centuries before the invention of the telescope. The scroll dates back to approximately 700 C.E., and its detail and accuracy are extraordinary."

JULIAN HARRISON
Lead Curator

▲ ▼

THE DUNHUANG STAR ATLAS (CHINA, CA. 700 C.E.)
British Library

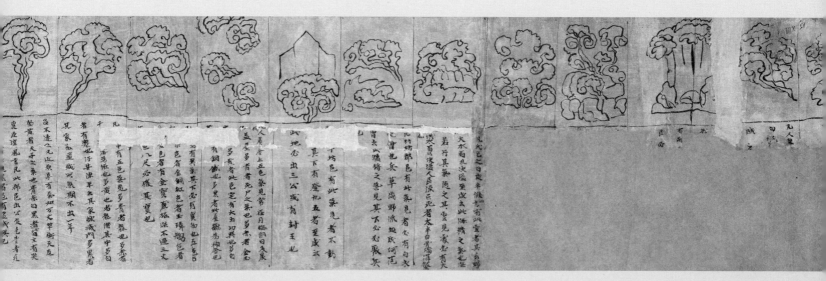

▶

**AN ASTRONOMICAL
MISCELLANY
(PETERBOROUGH, 12TH
CENTURY)**
British Library

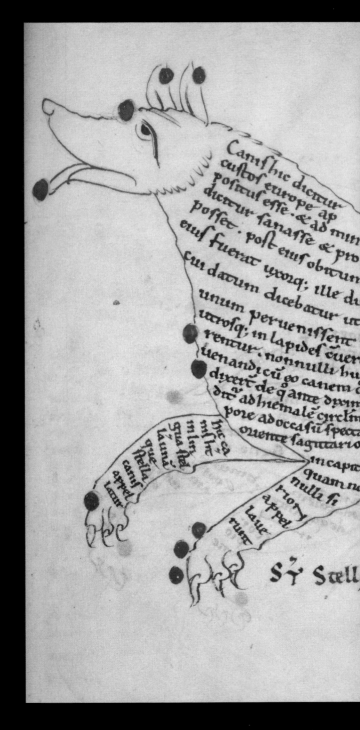

FOR ONE BRIEF MOMENT, THE GREAT BLACK DOG REARED ON TO ITS HIND LEGS AND PLACED ITS FRONT PAWS ON HARRY'S SHOULDERS, BUT MRS. WEASLEY SHOVED HARRY AWAY TOWARD THE TRAIN DOOR, HISSING, "FOR HEAVEN'S SAKE, ACT MORE LIKE A DOG, SIRIUS!"

—HARRY POTTER AND THE ORDER OF THE PHOENIX

Syrivs.

...uisse quem procris cephali uxori morbo laborantem
...canem munere acepisse ne ulla fera precurrere eum
...cephalum peruenit quod peris
...im peruenit thebas ibi erat uulpis
...anes effugere posset. itaq; cum in
nesciuf quid facere ut histrus ait
a beneficia aliq tempore degenera
outone dixert. & qd studiosus fuer g;
constituit. alii aut icarii canem ee
fugientem sequens. postioub; pedib' dui
tru orionis pene suo capite ciungens cor
ut equinoctialem circlin tendens. 7 occidens
utem cu cancro.

de q prius   tref. in sinistro lum
dixim? in   bo. 1. in pede poste
itrisq; aut   rioze .i. in pe
b' singtas ob   de dext
scuras in   .i. in
pectore.11   cauda
in pe   .v.
de pri   om
oze.111   nmo
utter   .xx.
sca
ptis

The wonders of the night sky have inspired many of the character names in the Harry Potter series. Hogwarts alumni include Andromeda Tonks, Bellatrix Lestrange, and of course their cousin, Sirius Black. This medieval manuscript shows the constellation of Canis Major. The most famous star in that constellation and also the brightest light that can be seen from Earth is Sirius, the Dog Star. The shape of the dog in this manuscript is infilled with a pattern poem in Latin, derived from the writings of the Roman author Hyginus.

ASTRONOMY

EYES TO THE SKIES

Astronomers of the past used a range of equipment to help them plot the movement of the stars. This exquisite instrument made by Muhammad b. Abi Bakr almost eight hundred years ago is called an astrolabe. It could be used to create a two-dimensional map of the heavens, similar to the star charts that Harry and his classmates were expected to plot in their Astronomy exams. An astrolabe was also able to determine latitude and was employed in the Islamic world to find the direction of Mecca. The back of this astrolabe has a calendar with three apertures including one showing the lunar phase and one the positions of the Sun and Moon in the zodiac. This astrolabe from Persia (modern day Iran) is thought to be one of the oldest existing geared instruments.

TURNING CIRCLES

Celestial globes show the position of stars in the sky as perceived from Earth. The art dates back thousands of years—the first celestial globes were created in ancient Greece. This example was designed by a Franciscan monk named Vincenzo Coronelli, considered to be one of the greatest globe makers in the world. Coronelli often collaborated with Jean Baptist Nolin, engraver to the French Crown. Working with draft maps provided by Coronelli, Nolin engraved beautiful baroque constellation figures of animals, men, and mythical creatures shown in constant dialogue as they move together across the sky. This globe also contains information about wind direction. Half of its emblem was left empty so that the makers could insert the name of the person to whom it was to be dedicated.

▲
MUHAMMAD B. ABI BAKR, ASTROLABE (ISFAHAN, 1221–22)
American Museum of Natural History Library

▶
VINCENZO CORONELLI, CELESTIAL GLOBE (VENICE, 1699)
Beinecke Rare Book and Manuscript Library, Yale University

MECHANICAL MAGIC

An orrery is a model of the solar system. This mechanical marvel was made in London by the mathematical instrument maker, John Troughton. It displays the movement of Earth in relation to the Moon and two other planets. The model rests on an octagonal wooden base, above which curves a series of bands marking celestial longitude and latitude. Orreries have long been used in teaching and were even available for purchase in Diagon Alley. At Hogwarts, they are not only used for Astronomy, but also for "planetary divination." Professor Sybill Trelawney's orrery holds "the moons [...] the nine planets and the fiery sun, all of them hanging in thin air beneath the glass."

HE WAS SORELY TEMPTED, TOO, BY THE PERFECT, MOVING MODEL OF THE GALAXY IN A LARGE GLASS BALL, WHICH WOULD HAVE MEANT HE NEVER HAD TO TAKE ANOTHER ASTRONOMY LESSON.

—*HARRY POTTER AND THE PRISONER OF AZKABAN*

▶ **MINIATURE ORRERY MADE BY JOHN TROUGHTON (LONDON, 18TH CENTURY)**
Science Museum

KEPLER ON THE STARS

Written by the imperial astronomer Johannes Kepler, the *Rudolphine Tables* helped its readers to locate the planets in relation to the stars. It was a massive achievement, containing the position of 1,005 stars, and is the most accurate star catalog of the pre-telescope era. The elaborate illustrated frontispiece of the book shows a temple of Urania, the Muse of Astronomy. The temple is filled with great star-gazers—Hipparchus of Nicaea, Ptolemy, Nicolaus Copernicus, Kepler's predecessor Tycho Brahe, and an unnamed Chaldean, an ancient people renowned for their astronomical skills. In a panel underneath the temple there is also a picture of Kepler himself.

"In 1617, Kepler's mother was suspected of witchcraft, a crime punishable by death. The accused spent over a year in prison but was eventually released when her son intervened. Kepler was an official astronomer to the Holy Roman Emperor—this family intrigue must have been very difficult for him."

ALEXANDER LOCK
Curator

▶

JOHANNES KEPLER, *TABULAE RUDOLPHINAE* (ULM, 1627)
British Library

LEONARDO ON THE MOON

Leonardo da Vinci—inventor, scientist, artist—
was centuries ahead of his time. Throughout his
career, Leonardo made notes written in curious
mirrored handwriting that reads from right to
left. Some of these pages were later gathered
into a notebook known as the "Codex Arundel,"
named after a former owner, the Earl of Arundel.
The shaded diagram in the center describes the
reflection of light, according to the alignments of
the Sun, Moon, and Earth. Leonardo's drawing
shows the Sun and Moon revolving around
the Earth, accepting the theory by the Greek
astronomer Ptolemy that the Earth was the center
of the universe. Leonardo also believed that the
Moon was covered with water and that its surface
would reflect light like a convex mirror.

▶
**LEONARDO DA VINCI'S
NOTEBOOK (ITALY,
CA. 1506–8)**
British Library

HARRY WATCHED THE CLOUDY SKY, CURVES OF SMOKE-GRAY AND SILVER SLIDING OVER THE FACE OF THE WHITE MOON. HE FELT LIGHT-HEADED WITH AMAZEMENT AT HIS DISCOVERIES.

—HARRY POTTER AND THE DEATHLY HALLOWS

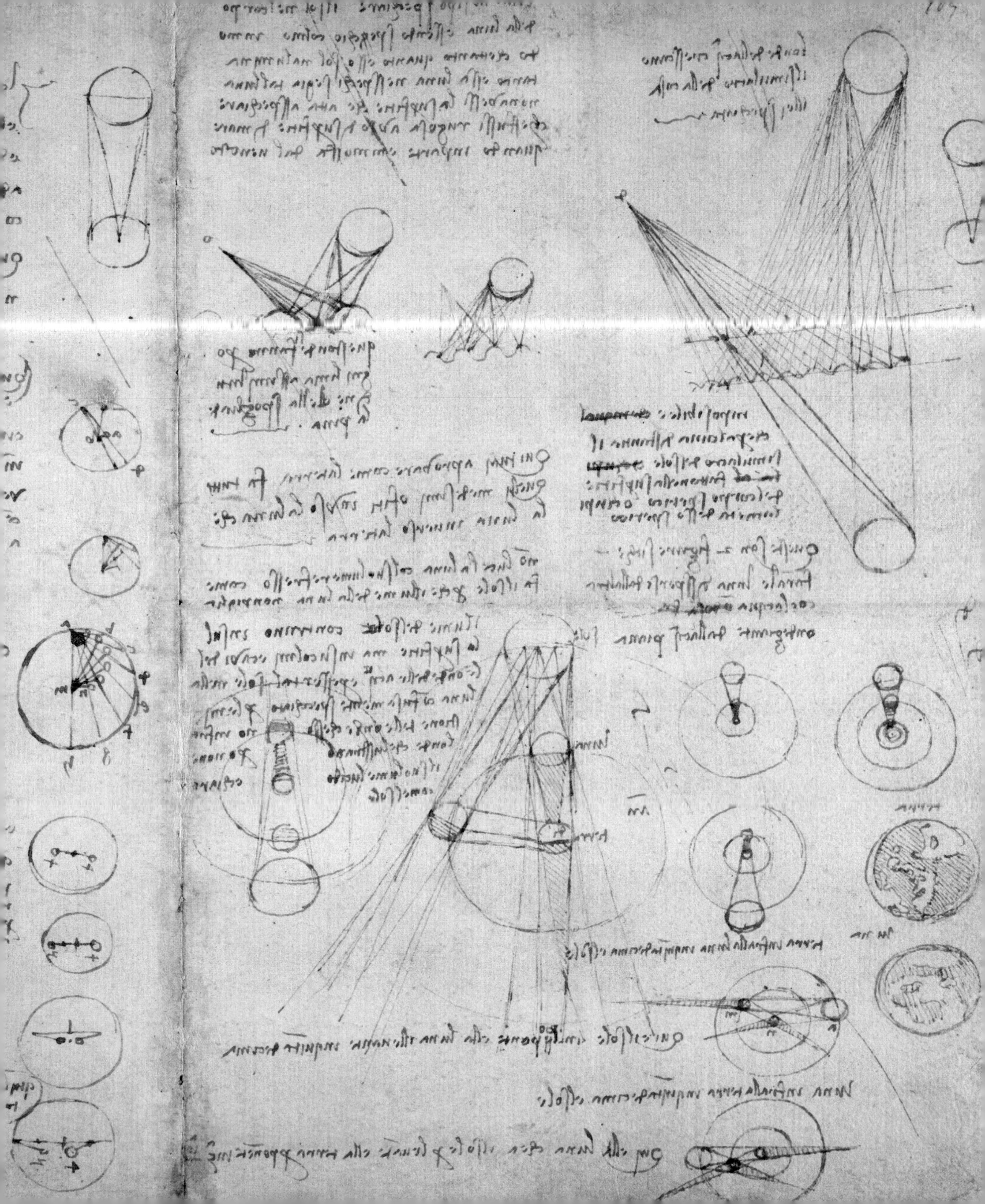

A VIEW OF THE HEAVENS

Just the thing for Hogwarts First Years, *Urania's Mirror* is a set of 32 star charts, printed on cardstock and sold for astronomical self-instruction. Each card is pierced with holes that correspond to the size of the brightest stars, giving a realistic impression of a constellation when held up to the light. The cards were engraved by the mapmaker Sidney Hall and then painted by hand. The images were designed by an anonymous "Lady," who has since been identified as the Reverend Richard Bloxam, an assistant master at Rugby School in Warwickshire, England. It is unclear why Bloxam hid his connection with these cards. Perhaps, like other authors, he felt that his gender might affect sales in a market that, at the time, wanted to attract female customers.

THEY BOUGHT HARRY'S SCHOOL BOOKS IN A SHOP CALLED FLOURISH AND BLOTTS WHERE THE SHELVES WERE STACKED TO THE CEILING WITH BOOKS AS LARGE AS PAVING STONES BOUND IN LEATHER . . .
—*HARRY POTTER AND THE SORCERER'S STONE*

▶ *URANIA'S MIRROR; OR A VIEW OF THE HEAVENS* (LONDON, 1834)
British Library

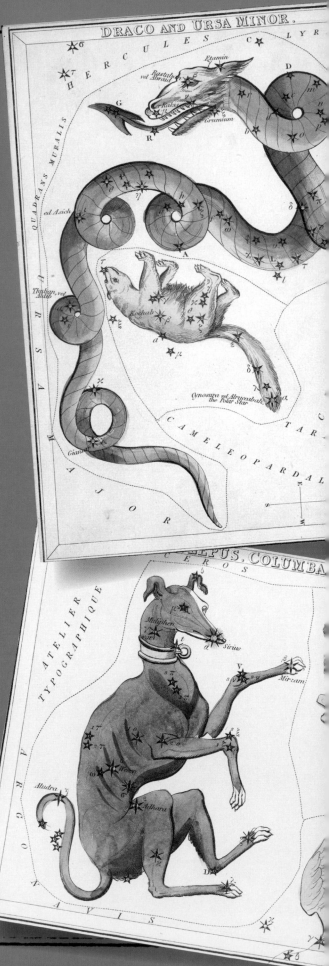

A SEAFARER'S STAR NOTES

Celestial navigation is the ancient science of finding your way by the position of the stars, Moon, and planets. Out of almost six thousand visible stars, only 58—the brightest—are used by navigators in their almanacs. This handwritten notebook, sometimes referred to as a commonplace book, has been filled with information on maritime navigation gathered from a variety of sources. The volume is wonderfully illustrated with working dials, tables, and other drawings that are both practical and eye-catching. Woodcuts from a 1710 issue of *The Ladies' Diary: or, the Woman's Almanack* complement its section on astronomy, and include northern hemisphere constellations Draco (the Dragon) and Cygnus (the Swan). The content of this notebook suggests that it dates from the early 18th century, and though it carries a bookplate of Cary Christopher Elwes, the son-in-law of a British rear admiral, the identity of its creator remains a mystery.

[...] HARRY LOOKED UPWARD AND SAW A VELVETY BLACK CEILING DOTTED WITH STARS. HE HEARD HERMIONE WHISPER, "IT'S BEWITCHED TO LOOK LIKE THE SKY OUTSIDE, I READ ABOUT IT IN *HOGWARTS: A HISTORY*."
—*HARRY POTTER AND THE SORCERER'S STONE*

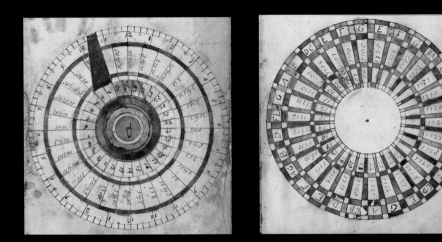

◀ ▶
A SEAFARER'S NAVIGATION NOTEBOOK, (UNITED STATES, 18TH CENTURY)
New-York Historical Society

ANother company of Stars that encompass the pole of ye Ecliptick @ lie dispersed in various places, the antients formed an Image or Constellation called ye Dragon (see fig 3) wreathing @ twisting it Self betwixt the two bears, it is a noble Constellation, having Stars in every one of ye 12 Signs @ the pole of ye Ecliptick is in the very middle of it, (at p) it hath one Star of ye Second Magnitude, (at s) being ye last but two in ye tail, the Star (at o) is called Rasaben, being a bright Star in the head of ye Dragon, famous for that ye Ingenious

Draco the Dragon
Fig. 3.

mr Robert Hook fellow of ye Royal Society, made use of this Star to attempt the Proof of the Motion of ye Earth by observation, in 1674 where he observed (as ye Reverend mr Flamsteed hath divers times since) a parallax of the Earths Annual orb which infallibly proves the motion of the Earth to be true, according to ye Doctrine of Copernicus

———— Behind the neck of the Dragon, the antients formed another Constellation of Stars into ye Image of a Swan (see fig 4) the Star near the Tail (at m) is of ye 2 Magnitude, @ is called Arides or Aridod; @ near the Star in its breast, where ye letter (n) is placed; a New Star appeared in the year 1601, @ after some time disappeared, in the year 1658 it appeared again, @ likewise in the year 1670, and so it continued appearing and disappearing several tim-

Cygnus the Swan
Fig. 4.

es, it was a Star of the third Magnitude, and at this time wholly Disappears

———— The Stars in this (as in ye other Constellations) are easily known & distinguished, if you observe about wt parts of ye Head, neck, Breast, Wings Tail &t, they are placed.

———— And this was ye method made use of by ye Antients, to distinguish @ Name ye greatest part of ye visable Stars in ye Firmament, by forming most of them into Images and Constellations

The
goods
Pre-
es. so
s. 7
wit.

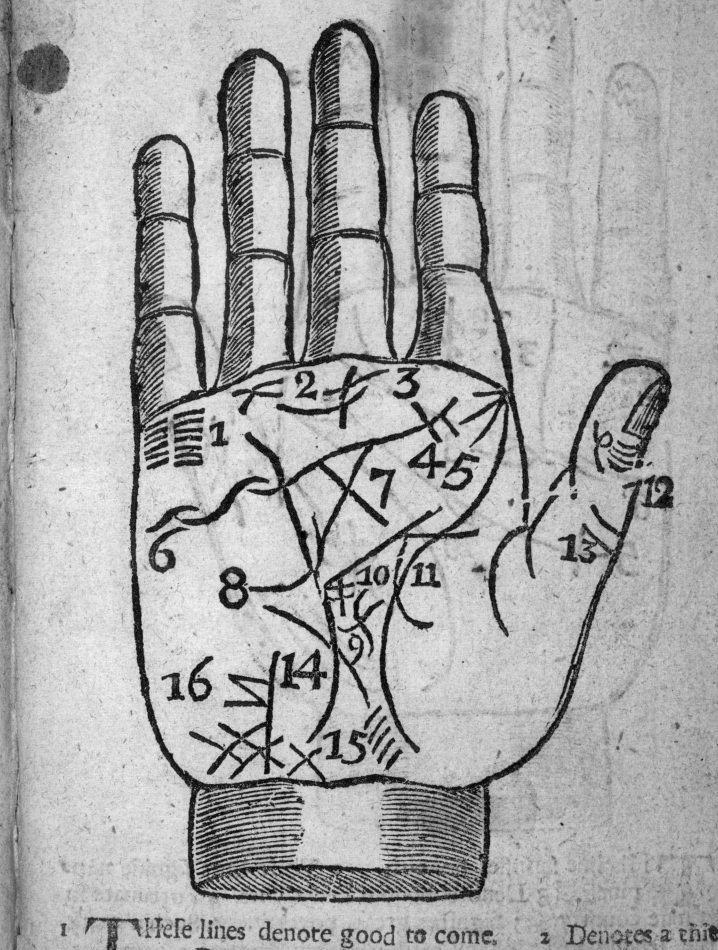

CHAPTER 6

DIVINATION

A TRUE SEER

Here is the completed portrait of Professor Sybill Trelawney, Harry Potter's Divination teacher at Hogwarts, wrapped in a shawl and dressed in her bangles and beads. To create this image Jim Kay painted an initial version in which Trelawney was not wearing her thick spectacles—the glasses and other elements were designed separately and added digitally later. The professor's fervent upward gaze captures how swept up she could become in the theatrics of her subject, in her view "the most difficult of all magical arts." The red glow of the Divination tower classroom behind her is visually evocative of a grand theater set.

"MY NAME IS PROFESSOR TRELAWNEY. YOU MAY NOT HAVE SEEN ME BEFORE. I FIND THAT DESCENDING TOO OFTEN INTO THE HUSTLE AND BUSTLE OF THE MAIN SCHOOL CLOUDS MY INNER EYE."

—PROFESSOR TRELAWNEY, *HARRY POTTER AND THE PRISONER OF AZKABAN*

▶ PORTRAIT OF SYBILL TRELAWNEY BY JIM KAY
Bloomsbury

CHINESE ORACLE BONES

Oracle bones were used in divination rituals associated with the cult of the ancestors in ancient China. Questions relating to subjects as mundane as a king's toothache to state affairs such as royal pregnancies, warfare, agriculture, and natural disasters would be engraved on the bone before heated metal sticks were inserted into pre-carved hollows, causing the bone to crack. The shaman then interpreted the patterns of the fractures to "receive the oracle" from the spirits of the ancestors. Oracle bones are archaeological evidence of China's earliest documented writing system, known as *jiaguwen*. These inscriptions are irrefutable historical records of a highly advanced civilization in China by the second millennium B.C.E., known as the Shang dynasty. The oxen shoulder blade on the left has been fragmented and bears an incomplete inscription, but the first graph from the top is clearly visible and denotes "divination." It is believed that the bone on the far right dates to the late Shang dynasty based on the ancient drill holes on the obverse side.

▲ ▶
ORACLE BONES
(CHINA, CA. 1600–
1046 B.C.E.)
Metropolitan Museum of Art

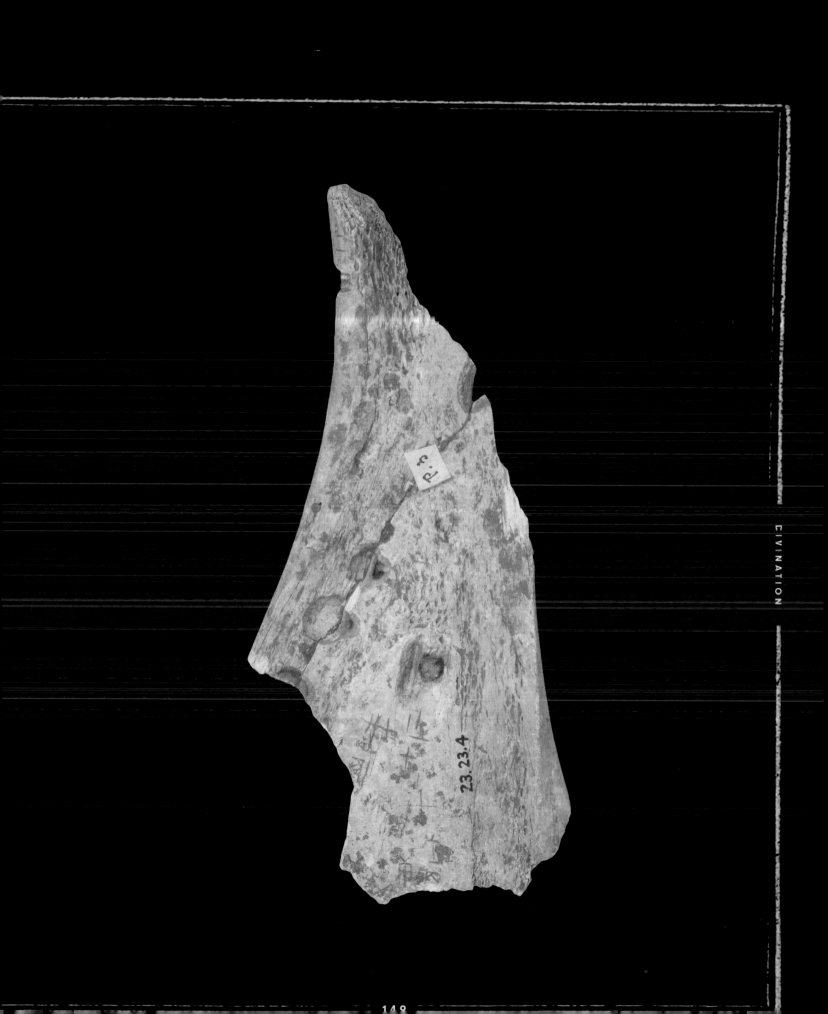

23.23.4

MOTHER SHIPTON

Mother Shipton, known as the Yorkshire Prophetess, is the subject of this little book. Little is known about her life, and we cannot even be sure that she existed. She was supposedly incredibly ugly, and in addition to her powers of prophecy she was able to levitate. Most of the "strange prophecies" in this book relate to the succession of the British monarchy, although Mother Shipton also predicted the day and time of her own death, reputedly in 1561. She appeared in various pamphlets from 1641 onward, and by the time this book was published in 1797, she was being portrayed in pantomimes on the London stage. Today, the prophetess is best known for her birthplace, which was said to be near the "Dropping Well" in Knaresborough, Yorkshire. For centuries the well was believed to have magical properties, and the capacity to turn objects into stone. The waters actually have a high mineral content, enabling them to petrify objects within a few weeks.

▲
WONDERS!!! PAST, PRESENT, AND TO COME; BEING THE STRANGE PROPHECIES AND UNCOMMON PREDICTIONS OF THE FAMOUS MOTHER SHIPTON (LONDON, 1797)
British Library

"Mother Shipton made her most famous prophecy in 1530, when she foretold that Cardinal Wolsey, who had been made Archbishop of York, would see the city but never reach it. According to this book, Wolsey saw the city from the top of a nearby castle, but was immediately arrested and taken to London."

TANYA KIRK
Curator

A WITCH'S SCRYING MIRROR

Divination with a mirror or another reflective surface is an ancient practice known as scrying. The term originates from the word "descry," meaning "to catch sight of." Despite being carved in the shape of an ugly, old hag, the design of this mirror was very popular among early 20th-century English witches, who would have used it for divination. This item once belonged to the witch Cecil Williamson. He warned that if you gaze into it, "and suddenly see someone standing behind you, whatever you do, do not turn around." The Mirror of Erised appears to act like a scrying mirror. It is equally dangerous too, as "It shows us nothing more or less than the deepest, most desperate desire of our hearts."

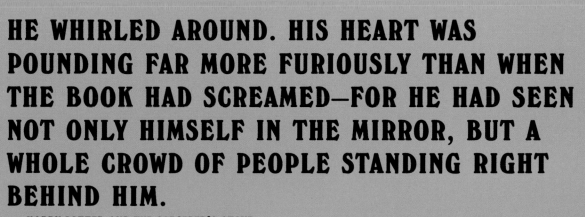

▶

A WOODEN WITCH'S MIRROR
*The Museum of Witchcraft and Magic,
Boscastle*

HE WHIRLED AROUND. HIS HEART WAS POUNDING FAR MORE FURIOUSLY THAN WHEN THE BOOK HAD SCREAMED—FOR HE HAD SEEN NOT ONLY HIMSELF IN THE MIRROR, BUT A WHOLE CROWD OF PEOPLE STANDING RIGHT BEHIND HIM.
—HARRY POTTER AND THE SORCERER'S STONE

THE ART OF CARTOMANCY

Cartomancy is a form of divination that uses cards to predict the future. Reading card decks for purposes of divination can be traced at least as far back as the 15th century but tarot cards, produced especially for fortune telling, became popular in Europe and North America during the 18th century. The modern tarot deck contains 78 cards divided into Minor and Major sections. Each card has a different meaning and arranged in spreads from 3 to 21 cards they tell the story of a person's life. *L'Ermite* or the Hermit represents soul-searching and introspection. *La Force* or Fortitude, portrayed by a woman subduing a lion, represents inner strength and resilience. Fifteen cards arranged in an upside down triangle create what is known as a Witch's Spread. The power of the message lies in the diviner as Harry Potter's teacher, Professor Trelawney, constantly tells her class.

▶ **HAND-COLORED TAROT CARDS (FRANCE, 18TH CENTURY)**
New-York Historical Society

ROY DE DENIER

TEN...

LA PAPESSE

IIX

LE PAPE

LUCKY IN LOVE?

In 19th-century Siam, people would have consulted
a divination specialist on matters of love and
relationships. This divination manual (*phrommachat*)
contains horoscopes based on the Chinese zodiac,
including drawings of the animals of the twelve-year
cycle and their reputed attributes—earth, wood,
fire, iron, and water. Each zodiac page is followed by
a series of paintings, which symbolize the fate of a
person under certain circumstances. The unnamed
artist paid great attention to every single detail: The
facial expressions, hand gestures and body language
are beautifully observed, along with the elaborate
designs of clothes and jewelry.

*"This manuscript describes both
lucky and unlucky constellations
for couples, taking into
consideration their characters
as well as their horoscopes.
Indeed, it would appear that a
hot-tempered couple would have
a better chance of living happily
together than a demonic male
and an angelic female."*

JANA IGUNMA
Curator

▶
**A THAI DIVINATION
MANUAL (*PHROMMACHAT*)
(SIAM, 19TH CENTURY)**
British Library

ๅก็กีชนะ:สยุเภาพรม
า๔เปนมือข้า๖เปน
เปน์คืนจัว ๑ เปนที
ปธาคุเหลกไปเสือผู้หย
ับางไก้เงอหาเภก
ปสเทวังก์ฤูบวคยกสง
ทย๚ก์ว่ามกอาภปัญ
รณาคันจ์นักแก ะ
คุเหลกคีเมือฺายมก
ภกรมักใต๋เปนไญูก์ว
รเมกสวๆๆสิใจยงฟสวน
ฺฒ์วาย๚
มกรายสร์มาายศี ทะ
กธาคุเหลกออนเมท
รกฎวายมิทิตถังงุเทาท์
รเมกสหๆสใจปูสูมิปัญ
ฺมาทย
ปนธาคเหลกกท์ราชกา
รเมกสวปๆแคก์๋ใท์หา
ฺมฺาทย
กเขใใจ แคว่าใใจ สิๆ
คฺฺนจ์นคนยากแก ะ
ธาคเหลกกคีท์าราชการ
ปฺญ์มิ เงนทอง เบาไฟ
ภฺคน
ก์ ๚คีมักเรฺ่ฆความ
ฺฆาย
มิปๅๆๅนักแก ะ

"I DO NOT EXPECT ANY OF YOU TO SEE WHEN FIRST YOU PEER INTO THE ORB'S INFINITE DEPTHS. WE SHALL START BY PRACTICING RELAXING THE CONSCIOUS MIND AND EXTERNAL EYES [...] PERHAPS, IF WE ARE LUCKY, SOME OF YOU WILL SEE BEFORE THE END OF THE CLASS."

—PROFESSOR TRELAWNEY, *HARRY POTTER AND THE PRISONER OF AZKABAN*

A PRACTICAL GUIDE TO

CRYSTAL GAZING

In the late 19th century, as interest in crystal divination increased, the clairvoyant John Melville wrote this popular guide to help those struggling with the ancient art. Melville recommended taking "an infusion of the herb *Mugwort* . . . or of the herb *Succory*," which, "if taken occasionally during the Moon's increase . . . [would] constitute an *aid* to the attainment of the most desirable *physical conditions* of the experimenter's body." It is unclear how far Melville's instructions helped those not gifted with Second Sight.

▶

JOHN MELVILLE,
*CRYSTAL GAZING AND THE
WONDERS OF CLAIRVOYANCE,
EMBRACING PRACTICAL
INSTRUCTIONS IN THE ART,
HISTORY, AND PHILOSOPHY
OF THIS ANCIENT SCIENCE,
2ND EDN (LONDON, 1910)*
British Library

SEEING THE FUTURE

Early in their Divination classes, the Hogwarts students were taught to divine using crystal balls. As Professor Trelawney recognized, "Crystal gazing is a particularly refined art." It was also an art that many of her students struggled to master. Harry "felt extremely foolish, staring blankly at the crystal ball," while Ron simply "made some stuff up." Crystallomancy has its roots in the Middle Ages, but this large ball is typical of the orbs consulted in the 19th and 20th centuries. It sits on an elaborate stand formed of three griffins at the base of an Egyptian-style column.

▶
A CRYSTAL BALL AND STAND
The Museum of Witchcraft and Magic, Boscastle

MAGIC JEWELS AND CRYSTAL BALLS

Since ancient times, certain stones and gems have been prized for their magical qualities. In *The Magic of Jewels & Charms*, George Kunz, chief gemologist for Tiffany & Co., chronicles the folklore of gemstones across time and place, from the magical stones used in rain-making rites by Central African tribes to the feldspar and quartz beach pebbles kept by Native Americans as talismans. Kunz's writings also explore the tradition of crystal gazing, the natural sources for rock crystal, and techniques for making crystal balls. Japanese artisans transformed rough masses of crystal into perfect spheres by painstakingly chipping them with small steel hammers and then grinding them to a fine polish, while in Europe and the US, workmen relied almost exclusively on huge mechanized grindstones to shape the balls.

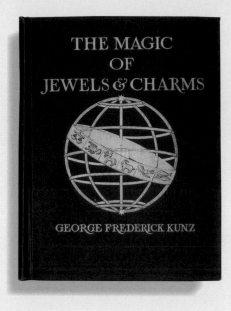

▲
GEORGE KUNZ, *THE MAGIC OF JEWELS & CHARMS* **(PHILADELPHIA, 1915)**
New-York Historical Society

SMELLY NELLY'S CRYSTAL BALL

Ron, Hermione, and Harry's Divination lessons took place in a heavily scented classroom, filled with a "sickly sort of perfume." "Smelly Nelly," the 20th-century English witch who owned this black crystal ball, also had a taste for strong aromas. One witness who saw her using it reported how, "You caught her scent a mile off downwind." Smelly Nelly believed that the fragrance appealed to the spirits who helped her to divine the future. Known as a Moon crystal, this black globe had to be consulted at night, so that the seer could read the Moon's reflection in the glass.

▶
A BLACK MOON CRYSTAL BALL
The Museum of Witchcraft and Magic, Boscastle

READING THE PALMS

Making a prediction based on the shape and lines of the hand is known as palmistry or chiromancy. This medieval manuscript contains a collection of prophecies and treatises on fortune-telling. Every hand contains three natural lines, forming a "triangle." These diagrams show a left and a right hand, onto which are mapped the natural lines and other secondary lines. On the right hand, a vertical stroke running down the palm reads, "this line represents love." A vertical line running between the middle and index finger has a less fortunate meaning: "This line signifies a bloody death and if the line reaches unto the middle of the finger it signifies a sudden death."

THE FIRST DIVINATION LESSON OF THE NEW TERM WAS MUCH LESS FUN; PROFESSOR TRELAWNEY WAS NOW TEACHING THEM PALMISTRY, AND SHE LOST NO TIME IN INFORMING HARRY THAT HE HAD THE SHORTEST LIFE LINE SHE HAD EVER SEEN.
—*HARRY POTTER AND THE PRISONER OF AZKABAN*

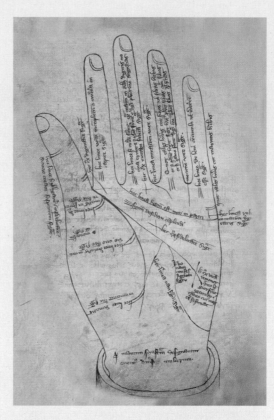

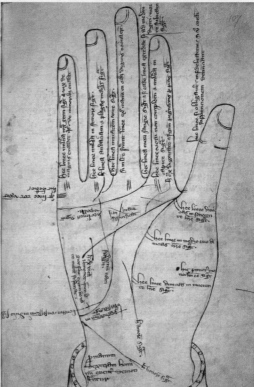

► **READING THE HANDS, IN A FORTUNE-TELLING MANUSCRIPT (ENGLAND, 14TH CENTURY)**
British Library

EVEN BY HARRY'S LOW STANDARDS IN DIVINATION, THE EXAM WENT VERY BADLY. . . . [HE] ROUNDED OFF THE WHOLE FIASCO BY MIXING UP THE LIFE AND HEAD LINES ON HER PALM AND INFORMING HER THAT SHE OUGHT TO HAVE DIED THE PREVIOUS TUESDAY.

—*HARRY POTTER AND THE ORDER OF THE PHOENIX*

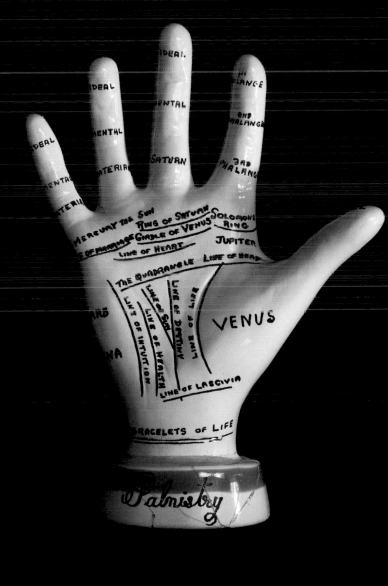

A PALMISTRY HAND

This ceramic palmistry hand would have been used for teaching. It shows the various lines and mounts on the palm and wrist, along with some of their significant meanings. Hands like this were first manufactured in Britain in the 1880s, following the growing popularity of palmistry inspired by the celebrated astrologer William John Warner, also known as Cheiro or Count Louis Hamon.

◀

A PALMISTRY HAND
The Museum of Witchcraft and Magic, Boscastle

THE OLD EGYPTIAN FORTUNE-TELLER'S LAST LEGACY

This fascinating 18th-century pamphlet explores, and perhaps exploits, Egypt's mystical reputation. Supposedly a collection of Egyptian divination techniques, it was compiled by an anonymous British writer. *The Old Egyptian Fortune-Teller's Last Legacy* was printed cheaply and then sold to the lower middle classes. In addition to palmistry, it explains how to prick an image with a pin to decide whom to marry and how to divine the future by interpreting the moles on your face and body. Even the position and number of your wrinkles are deemed to hold secrets to the future.

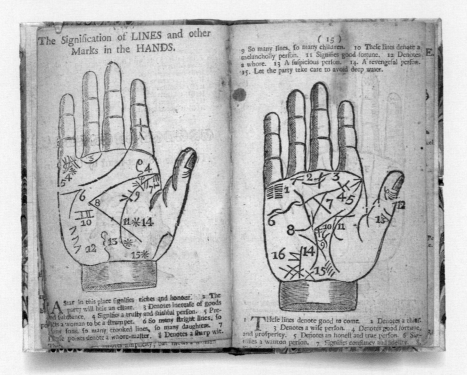

◄ THE OLD EGYPTIAN FORTUNE-TELLER'S LAST LEGACY (LONDON, 1775)
British Library

"HERE YOU ARE," SAID THE MANAGER, WHO HAD CLIMBED A SET OF STEPS TO TAKE DOWN A THICK, BLACK-BOUND BOOK. "*UNFOGGING THE FUTURE.* VERY GOOD GUIDE TO ALL YOUR BASIC FORTUNE-TELLING METHODS—PALMISTRY, CRYSTAL BALLS, BIRD ENTRAILS . . ."

—*HARRY POTTER AND THE PRISONER OF AZKABAN*

LADY FATE

From the late 18th to the early 20th centuries, doll owners sometimes converted their little charges into fortune-tellers. They were a party novelty and a money-making feature at charity bazaars and local fairs, where the curious paid to take their turn. Plucking one of the skirt's folded paper leaves yields a flowery fortune relating to love, friendship, and personality, such as "beware the man that flatters you." A few of the handwritten messages in this example come from the *Oraculum*, an oracle papyrus that Napoleon Bonaparte purportedly discovered in Egypt. Though undoubtedly a hoax, English-language publishers reprinted it through the 19th century. A range of doll bodies, from porcelain to papier-mâché, found themselves transformed into fortune-tellers. This type, known as a "peg wooden," hails from the historic wood-carving center of Val Gardena (Grödental) in the South Tyrol region, then part of Austria and today in Northern Italy.

▶

A FORTUNE-TELLING DOLL (DOLL: VAL GARDENA, CA. 1825; CLOTHING: ENGLAND OR UNITED STATES, MID-19TH CENTURY)
New-York Historical Society

A FORTUNE-TELLING TEACUP

Tasseography—from the French *tasse* (cup) and Greek *graph* (writing)—is a form of divination that interprets the sediment in cups, usually left by tea leaves. The location and shape of the tea leaves left in the cup have different symbolism. The first European accounts of this method of divination appeared in the 17th century, following the introduction of tea from China. This delicate pink divination cup was made in the 1930s by Paragon, an English manufacturer of bone china. The inside of the cup has been decorated with symbols to help interpret the leaves. A legend runs around the rim: "Many curious things I see when telling fortunes in your tea."

◀ ▼

A FORTUNE-TELLING CUP AND
SAUCER MADE BY PARAGON
(STOKE-ON-TRENT, CA. 1932–39)
The Museum of Witchcraft and Magic, Boscastle

"[...] DRINK UNTIL ONLY THE DREGS REMAIN.
SWILL THESE AROUND THE CUP THREE TIMES
WITH THE LEFT HAND, THEN TURN THE CUP
UPSIDE DOWN ON ITS SAUCER; WAIT FOR THE
LAST OF THE TEA TO DRAIN AWAY, THEN GIVE
YOUR CUP TO YOUR PARTNER TO READ."

—PROFESSOR TRELAWNEY, *HARRY POTTER AND THE PRISONER OF AZKABAN*

A HIGHLAND SEER

This detailed manual on tea leaf divination was written by an unnamed author, described on the cover as "a Highland Seer." It provides instructions not only on interpreting the various shapes made by the leaves, but also on the ideal size and shape of cup and the type of tea to use.

▶

TEA CUP READING: HOW TO TELL FORTUNES BY TEA LEAVES BY A HIGHLAND SEER (TORONTO, CA. 1920)
British Library

"In this book, the position of each tea leaf symbol is also significant. The author advises that the nearer an image appears to the handle of the cup, the sooner the predicted event will occur."

TANYA KIRK
Curator

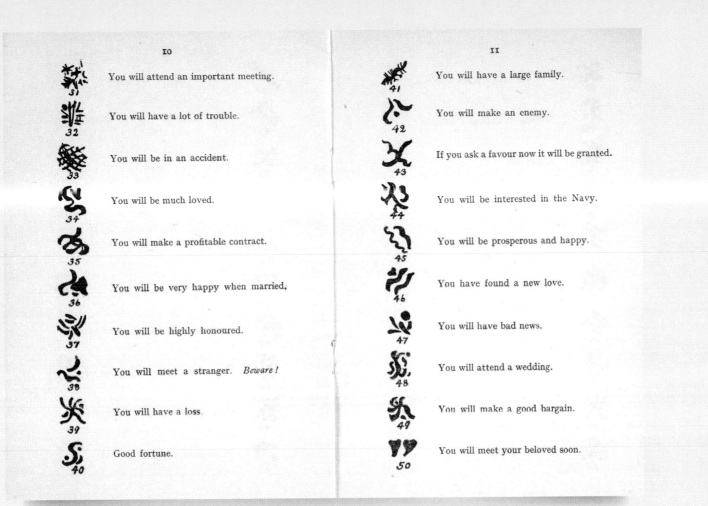

10

You will attend an important meeting.

You will have a lot of trouble.

You will be in an accident.

You will be much loved.

You will make a profitable contract.

You will be very happy when married.

You will be highly honoured.

You will meet a stranger. *Beware!*

You will have a loss.

Good fortune.

11

You will have a large family.

You will make an enemy.

If you ask a favour now it will be granted.

You will be interested in the Navy.

You will be prosperous and happy.

You have found a new love.

You will have bad news.

You will attend a wedding.

You will make a good bargain.

You will meet your beloved soon.

READING TEA LEAVES

This slim volume on tea leaf divination traces the first use of tasseography all the way back to 229 B.C.E. In that year, a Chinese princess rejected astrological predictions in favor of a new technique proposed by a student, using a popular beverage. The prophecies she obtained using tea leaves were so accurate that she "raised the fortunate cup reader to the dignity of a Mandarin" (a significant promotion!). Most of the pamphlet comprises a handy guide to decoding a range of shapes formed by leaves in the bottom of the cup. Many of the predictions are quite general; others are bizarrely specific. Number 44, for instance, indicates, "You will be interested in the Navy." Readers struggling with this volume might sympathize with Harry Potter, who could only see "A load of soggy brown stuff."

▲
HOW TO READ THE FUTURE WITH TEA LEAVES, TRANSLATED FROM THE CHINESE BY MANDRA (STAMFORD, CA. 1925)
British Library

"Some of the shapes in this book are remarkably difficult to tell apart. Numbers 38 and 42 are tantalizingly similar, but while the first means 'You will meet a stranger,' the other warns that 'You will make an enemy.'"

TANYA KIRK
Curator

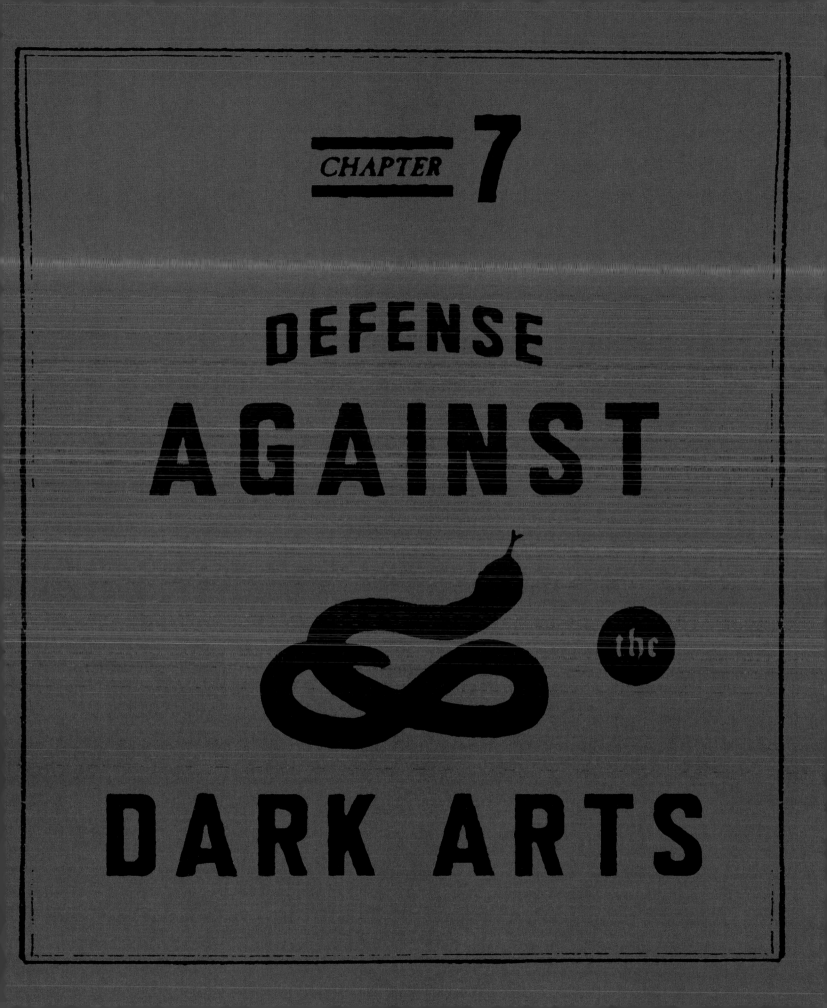

CHAPTER 7

DEFENSE AGAINST the DARK ARTS

HARRY ARRIVES AT PRIVET DRIVE

This original drawing by J.K. Rowling depicts the black night when Harry Potter was delivered to the Dursleys. With only the Moon and stars to light the way, since Dumbledore had put out the streetlamps with his Deluminator, Privet Drive is not visible. The giant Hagrid, still wearing his motorcycle goggles, stoops down to show baby Harry Potter to Dumbledore and Minerva McGonagall. Harry is the central focus of this image, wrapped in a white blanket, shining as brightly as the Moon. As the group contemplates the baby, Dumbledore's forehead is creased with concern. Professor McGonagall clasps her hands together, her hair drawn back in a tight bun. This quiet, dark moment was the beginning of Harry's story, fresh from his first encounter with Lord Voldemort.

FOR A FULL MINUTE THE
THREE OF THEM STOOD
AND LOOKED AT THE
LITTLE BUNDLE; HAGRID'S
SHOULDERS SHOOK,
PROFESSOR MCGONAGALL
BLINKED FURIOUSLY, AND
THE TWINKLING LIGHT
THAT USUALLY SHONE
FROM DUMBLEDORE'S EYES
SEEMED TO HAVE GONE
OUT.
—HARRY POTTER AND THE SORCERER'S STONE

▶

DRAWING OF HARRY
POTTER, DUMBLEDORE,
McGONAGALL, AND HAGRID
BY J.K. ROWLING
J.K. Rowling

A MYSTERIOUS MAN

This portrait shows Professor Lupin, Harry Potter's Defense Against the Dark Arts teacher. Remus Lupin only taught Harry during his third year at Hogwarts, resigning after Snape informed the students' parents about the professor's "furry little problem." Lupin, of course, was a werewolf. Lupin's lessons offered instruction on shape-shifting Boggarts and demonic Grindylows, and it was he who taught Harry to cast a Patronus for the first time. In this portrait, Lupin stands with his hands in his pockets, averting his gaze from the reader. The dark rings under his eyes and graying hair perhaps make him look older than he really is. The professor stands in his office, a bookcase behind him loaded with bottles, books, and bones. A poster of the Full Moon hangs on the shelves, representing the thing he fears the most.

▲

A PORTRAIT OF PROFESSOR REMUS LUPIN BY JIM KAY
Bloomsbury

"The grayscale coloring lends a solemn air to this beguiling picture. Despite being persecuted by the wizarding community, Lupin was one of Harry's closest links to his deceased father."

JOANNA NORLEDGE
Curator

HE PUSHED HIS GRAYING HAIR OUT OF HIS EYES, THOUGHT FOR A MOMENT, THEN SAID, "THAT'S WHERE ALL OF THIS STARTS—WITH MY BECOMING A WEREWOLF. NONE OF THIS COULD HAVE HAPPENED IF I HADN'T BEEN BITTEN . . . AND IF I HADN'T BEEN SO FOOLHARDY . . ."

—PROFESSOR LUPIN, *HARRY POTTER AND THE PRISONER OF AZKABAN*

BEWARE THE WEREWOLF

Johann Geiler von Kaysersberg was a theologian who preached at Strasbourg Cathedral in France. In 1508, he gave a series of sermons for Lent, which were transcribed and decorated with woodcut illustrations. The collection was later posthumously published as *Die Emeis* (*The Ants*). On the third Sunday of Lent ("Oculi"), Geiler delivered a sermon on werewolves. While Professor Snape may not have wished "to fathom the way a werewolf's mind works," Geiler listed seven reasons why such beasts could attack—including hunger, savageness, old age, and madness. He also advised that the likelihood of being bitten was affected by a werewolf's age and its experience of eating human flesh.

"If he were in charge, Geiler would never have allowed
a werewolf like Professor Lupin anywhere near
Hogwarts School. According to his sermon, werewolves
were dangerous beasts that especially liked to eat
children."
ALEXANDER LOCK
Curator

JOHANN GEILER VON
KAYSERSBERG, *DIE*
EMEIS (STRASBOURG,
1516.)
British Library

A SERPENTINE WAND

Snakes have long been considered magical creatures with great symbolic power. The ability of snakes to shed and regrow their skin is integral to their association with renewal, rebirth, and healing. In many cultures, snakes also represent good and evil, a dualism that has importance for their connection with magic. As Professor Dumbledore recognized in the Harry Potter books, anyone who associates with snakes is "supposedly connected with the Dark Arts, although as we know, there are Parselmouths among the great and the good too." The slender, serpentine wand at left was a tool for channeling magical forces— its dark color and snakelike shape force us to question whether it was used for good or for evil.

◀

A WAND SHAPED LIKE A SNAKE
The Museum of Witchcraft and Magic, Boscastle

A SERPENT STAFF

This magic staff was carved from bog oak: timber that had been buried for centuries in peat. The low oxygen levels, acidity, and tannins of the peat preserved the wood, hardening and blackening it in the process. It was carved by the Neopagan Stephen Hobbs and given to a Wiccan priest named Stewart Farrar during the late 20th century. The staff is almost six feet long and has been decorated with a serpent in order to enhance its power. Not only do snakes represent a capacity for change, renewal, and transformation, but their coils symbolize the dual cycles of light and dark, life and death, reason and passion, healing and poison, protection and destruction.

▶

A SERPENT STAFF
The Museum of Witchcraft and Magic, Boscastle

A SNAKE CHARMER

This image of a "wizard" charming a serpent is found in a beautifully illustrated bestiary. The accompanying text describes several mythological snakes, including the *cerastes* (a horned serpent) and the *scitalis* (a creature with incredible markings on its back). It then focuses on the *emorroris*, a type of asp so called because its bite causes hemorrhages of such disastrous proportions a victim will sweat out their own blood until they die. Fortunately, the manuscript explains one way to avoid such a fate. If a conjurer sings to the asp in its cave and lulls it to sleep, the snake charmer will then be able to remove the precious stone that grows on the asp's forehead. Without the stone, the snake is rendered powerless.

"The thick gold leaf in this bestiary bathes the page in light. The manuscript contains a further 80 illustrations of various real and mythical creatures, such as the phoenix, the unicorn, and the centaur."

JULIAN HARRISON
Lead Curator

▶

IMAGE OF A SNAKE CHARMER, IN A BESTIARY (ENGLAND, 13TH CENTURY)
British Library

"DINNER, NAGINI," SAID VOLDEMORT SOFTLY, AND THE GREAT SNAKE SWAYED AND SLITHERED FROM HIS SHOULDERS ONTO THE POLISHED WOOD.

—*HARRY POTTER AND THE DEATHLY HALLOWS*

SSSSSNAKES ALIVE!

Albertus Seba was a Dutch apothecary and collector, based in Amsterdam. From this center of maritime trade, Seba supplied drugs to the Russian Tsar Peter the Great. He also provided the port's ships with medicines, which he often traded for exotic animal specimens. After selling his first collection of snakes, birds, and lizards to the Tsar in 1717, Seba began a second, larger collection, which he kept in his own house. In 1731, he commissioned artists to draw every single item in precise detail. This was such a huge undertaking the project was not completed until 30 years after Seba's death and the volume contained 449 illustrated plates. Many of the specimens Seba collected were used for medical research. He took a keen interest in the potential of snakes for lifesaving cures—his collection contained many serpents such as this reticulated python, native to Southeast Asia.

◀

ALBERTUS SEBA, *LOCUPLETISSIMI RERUM NATURALIUM THESAURI ACCURATA DESCRIPTIO, ET INCONIBUS ARTIFICIOSISSIMIS EXPRESSIO, PER UNIVERSAM PHYSICES HISTORIAM, 4 VOLS* (AMSTERDAM, 1734–65)
British Library

THE "RED-EYED DWARF"

These typed pages are part of an early draft of *Harry Potter and the Sorcerer's Stone*. In this scene, Hagrid comes to the office of Fudge, a Muggle minister, and warns him about You-Know-Who (even in this early draft Hagrid refuses to say the name). In turn, Fudge warns the public about this "red-eyed dwarf." The red eyes remain in the final incarnation of Lord Voldemort, but the character took time to develop fully into the terrifying figure we now know from the published stories. This scene is reminiscent of Cornelius Fudge visiting the Prime Minister of the Muggles in the first chapter of *The Half-Blood Prince*. As J.K. Rowling has said, "I often cut ideas and put them into later books. Never waste a good scene!"

"Your kind?"

"Yeah... our kind. We're the ones who've bin disappearin'. We're all in hidin' now." But I can't tell yeh much abou' us. Can't 'ave Muggles knowin' our business. But this is gettin' outta hand, an' all you Muggles are gettin' involved - them on the train, fer instance - they shouldn'ta bin hurt like that. That's why Dumbledore sent me. Says it's your business too, now."

"You've come to tell me why all these houses are disappearing?" Fudge said, "And why all these people are being killed?"

"Ah, well now, we're not sure they 'ave bin killed," said the giant. "He's jus' taken them. Needs 'em, see. 'E's picked on the best. Dedalus Diggle, Elsie Bones, Angus an' Elspeth McKinnon ... yeah, 'e wants 'em on 'is side."

"You're talking about this little red-eyed -?"

"Shh!" hissed the giant. "Not so loud! 'E could be 'ere now, fer all we know!"

Fudge shuddered ~~shivered~~ and looked wildly aroudn them. "C - could he?"

"S'alright, I don' reckon I was followed," said the giant in a gravelly whisper.

"But who is this person? What is he? One of - um - your kind?"

The giant snorted.

"Was once, I s'pose," he said. "But I don' think 'e's anything yeh could put a name to any more. 'E's not a 'uman, ~~'E is not an animal. 'E is not properly.~~ Wish 'e was. 'E could be killed if 'e was still 'uman enough."

"He can't be killed?" whispered Fudge in terror. "'E's gotta be stopped, see?"

"Well, we don' think so. But Dumbledore's workin' on it."

"Well, yes of course," said Fudge. "We can't have this sort of thing going on..."

"This is nothin'," said the giant, "'E's just gettin' started. Once 'e's got the power, once 'e's got the followers, no-one'll be safe. Not even Muggles. I 'eard 'e'll keep yeh alive, though. Fer slaves."

Fudge's eyes bulged with terror.

~~But who is this — this person?~~

"This Bumblebore - Dunderbore -"

"Albus Dumbledore," said the the giant severely.

"Yes, yes, him - you say he has a plan?"

"Oh, yeah. So it's not hopeless yet. Reckon Dumbledore's the only one ~~he~~ "He's still afraid of. But 'e needs your 'elp. I'm 'ere teh

""Oh dear," said Fudge breathlessly, "The thing is, I'd be ~~was planning to retire early. Tomorrow, as a matter of fact. Mrs. Fudge and I were thinking of moving to Portugal. We have a villa-"

The giant lent forward, his beetle brows low over his glinting eyes.

"Yeh won' be safe in Portugal if 'e ain' stopped, Fudge."

"Won't I?" said Fudge weakly, "Oh, very well then... what is it Mr. Dumblething wants?"

"Dumbledore," said the giant. "Three things. First, yeh gotta put out a message. On television, an' radio, an' in the newspapers. Warn people not teh give 'im directions. 'Cause that's 'ow 'e's gettin' us, see? 'E 'as ter be told. Feeds on betrayal. I don' blame the Muggles, mind, they didn' know what they were doin'.

"Second, ~~yeh gotta make sure~~ ye're not teh tell anyone abou' us. If Dumbledore manages ter get rid of 'im, yeh gotta swear not ter go spreadin' it about what yeh know, abou' us. We keeps ourselves quiet, see? Let it stay that way.

"An' third, yeh gotta give me a drink before I go. I gotta long journey back."

The giant's face creased into a grin behind his wild beard.

"Oh - yes, of course," said Fudge shakily, "Help yourself - there's brandy up there - and - not that I suppose it will happen - I mean, I'm a Muddle - a Muffle - no, a Muggle - but if this person - this thing - comes looking for me -?"

"Yeh'll be dead," said the giant flatly over the top of a large glass of brandy. "No-one can survive if 'e attacks them. Ain' never been a survivor. But like yeh say, yer a Muggle. 'E's not interested in you."

The giant drained his glass and stood up. He pulled out an umbrealla. It was pink and had flowers on it.

"I'll be off, then," he said.

"Just one thing," said Fudge, watching curiously as the giant opened the umbrella, "What is this - person's - name."

The giant looked suddenly scared.

"Can' tell yeh that," he said, "We never say it. Never."

He raised the pink umbrella over his head, Fudge blinked - and the giant was gone.

* * * * *

▼
AN EARLY DRAFT OF HARRY POTTER AND THE SORCERER'S STONE
J.K. Rowling

"While many details of the world described in this chapter are familiar from the published books, such as the concept of Muggles, these scenes provide a very different account of the beginning of the story."

JOANNA NORLEDGE
Curator

Fudge wondered, of course, if he was going …? … no seriously considerd the possibility … the giant had been a hallucination. But the … glass the giant had drunk from was real enough, left standing on his desk.

Fudge wouldn't let his secretary remove the glass next day. It reassured him he wasn't a lunatic to do what he knew he had to do. He telephoned all the journalists he knew, and all the television stations, chose his favourite tie and gave a press conference. He told the world there was a ~~maniac madman~~ about a strange little man going about. A little man with red eyes. He told the public to be very careful not to tell this little man where anyone lived. Once he had given out this strange message, he said "Any questions?" But the room was completely silent. Clearly, they all thought he was off his rocker. Fudge went back to his office and sat staring at the giant's empty brandy glass. ~~This was the end of his career.~~

The very last person he wanted to see was Vernone Dursley. Dursley woudl be delighted. Dursley would be happily counting the days until he was made Minister, now that Fudge was so nearly nuttier than a bag of salted peanuts.

But Fudge had another surprise in store. Dursley knocked …ctly, came into his office, sat opposite him and said …atly,

You've had a visit from One of Them haven't you?"

"~~One of~~ Fudge looked at Dursley in amazement.

"You - know?"

"Yes," said Dursley bitterly, "I've known from the start. I happened to know there were people like that. Of course, …ever told anyone.

* * * * *

~~Most peop~~
~~Perhaps people did~~ most people did think Fudge

Whether or not nearly everyone thought Fudge had gone very …ge, the fact was that he seemed to have stopped the odd …ents. Three whole weeks passed, and still the empty brandy …stood on Fudge's desk to give him courage, and not one …lew, the houses of Britain stayed where they were, the … stopped going swimming. Fudge, who hadn't even told …udge about the giant with the pink umbrella, waited and …and slept with his fingers crossed. Surely this …dore would send a message if they'd managed to get rid …red eyed dwarf? Or did this horrible silence mean that …rf had in fact got everyone he wanted, that he was even …nning to appear in Fudge's office and vanish him too …to help the other side - whoever they were?

…d then - one Tuesday -

Later that evening, when everyone else had gone home, Dursley sneaked up to Fudge's office carrying a crib, which he laid on Fudge's desk.

The child was asleep. Fudge peered nervously into the crib. The boy had a cut on his forehead. It was a very strangely shaped cut. It looked like a bolt of lightening.

"Going to leave a scar, I expect," said Fudge.

"Never mind the ruddy scar, what are we going to do with him?" said Dursley.

"Do with him? Why, you'll have to take him home, of course," said Fudge in surprise. "He's your nephew. His parents have vanished. What else can we do? I thought you didn't want anyone to know you had relatives involved in all these odd doings."

"Take him home!" said Dursley in horror. "My son Didsbury is just this age, I don't want him coming in contact with one of these -"

"Very well, then, Dursley, we shall just have to try and find someone who does want to take him. Of course, it will be difficult to keep the story out of the press. Noone else has lived after one of these vanishments. There'll be a lot of interest -"

"Oh, very well," snapped Dursley angrily from the room.

He picked up the crib and stumped angrily from the room. It was time he was getting home too. He had just put his hand on the doorhandle when a low cough behind him made him clap his hand to his heart.

"Don't hurt me! I'm a Muggle! I'm a Muggle!"

"I know you are," said a low growling voice.

It was the giant.

"You!" said Fudge. "What is it? Oh, Good Lord, don't tell me-" For the giant, he saw, was crying. Sniffing into a large spotted handkerchief.

"It's all over," said Fudge faintly, "It didn't work? Was he not-" "Over?" said Fudge faintly, "It didn't work? Was he not turned into slaves?"

Dunderbore? Are we all going to be turned into slaves?"

"No, no," sobbed the giant. "He's gone. Everyone's come back. Diggle, the Bones, the McKinnons... they're all back. Safe. Everyone 'e took is back on our side an' He's disappeared 'imself."

"Good Heavens! This is wonderful news! You mean Mr. Dunderbumble's plan worked? "He's gone. Everyone's come back.

"Over?" said Fudge faintly, "It didn't work?

"Good Heavens! This is wonderful news! You mean Mr. Dunderbumble's plan worked?" This is wonderful news! You mean Mr. Dunderbumble's plan worked?" said the giant, mopping his eyes. "Never 'ad a chance to try it," said the giant, mopping his eyes.

AN ILLUSTRATOR'S FAVORITE WORK

Mary GrandPré considered *Harry Potter and the Deathly Hallows* to be her most favorite cover. It depicts a fiery orange sky, cracks in the battered walls of Hogwarts, and eerie shadows that create a backdrop for the ultimate confrontation between the Boy Who Lived and the Dark Lord. Near the center of the cover, the resurrected Harry is captured in the moment he defeats Voldemort once and for all.

▲
JACKET ART FOR *HARRY POTTER AND THE DEATHLY HALLOWS*
BY MARY GRANDPRÉ (2007)
Warner Bros.

HARRY AND THE BASILISK

Salazar Slytherin's monster, the giant basilisk, is shown coiling past Harry in this striking image from *The Chamber of Secrets*. The beast is so huge, it is hard to tell where its body begins or ends, and the dark colors of its scales are oppressive and intimidating. Harry is clutching the ruby-decorated sword of Godric Gryffindor in his hands, frozen in the air mid-swing. The bright white tip of the sword mirrors the sharp teeth of the basilisk. The monster's terrible yellow eyes are streaming with blood after Fawkes the phoenix has pierced them with its beak. This is an intense picture full of action and danger.

THE BASILISK'S HEAD WAS FALLING, ITS BODY COILING AROUND, HITTING PILLARS AS IT TWISTED TO FACE HIM. HE COULD SEE THE VAST, BLOODY EYE SOCKETS, SEE THE MOUTH STRETCHING WIDE, WIDE ENOUGH TO SWALLOW HIM WHOLE, LINED WITH FANGS LONG AS HIS SWORD, THIN, GLITTERING, VENOMOUS . . .

—*HARRY POTTER AND THE CHAMBER OF SECRETS*

◀ HARRY POTTER AND THE BASILISK BY JIM KAY
Bloomsbury

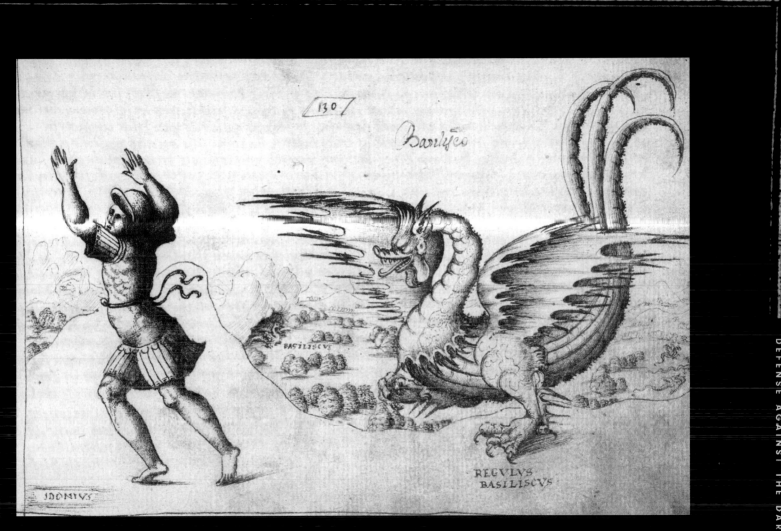

130

Basilisco

BASILISCVS

REGVLVS
BASILISCVS

IDOMIVS

A BRIEF DESCRIPTION OF THE BASILISK

This very *Brief Description*, comprising only a title page and two pages of text, was written by Jacobus Salgado. Salgado was a refugee from Spain and a convert to Protestantism, who came to settle in England. Around 1680, in need of cash, Salgado displayed a "basilisk" given to him by a Dutch doctor who had recently returned from Ethiopia. The creature presumably had been stuffed or preserved in some way. Salgado wrote this pamphlet to accompany the spectacle, describing the beast as yellow, with a crown-like crest and the body of a rooster attached to a serpent's tail. The pamphlet also spells out the danger of the basilisk's glare. Salgado declares that "In the time of Alexander the Great, there was one of them which, lying hid in a wall, killed a great troop of his soldiers by the poisonous glances of his eyes upon them."

"Despite Salgado's terrifying description of the basilisk, the creature on the title page looks rather harmless, even though it has just killed the person in the foreground."

TANYA KIRK
Curator

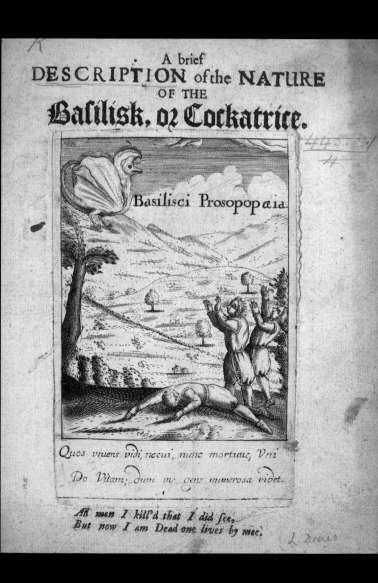

► JACOBUS SALGADO, A BRIEF DESCRIPTION OF THE NATURE OF THE BASILISK, OR COCKATRICE (LONDON, CA. 1680)
British Library

THE SPHINX

The Historie of Foure-Footed Beastes was the first major book about animals to be published in English. It features a variety of animals, from the common (rabbits, sheep, goats) to the exotic (lions, elephants, rhinoceroses) and the legendary. This chapter focuses on the sphinx. The woodcut illustration shows a creature with a woman's head and a lion's body. Edward Topsell described the sphinx as "of a fierce but tameable nature." Less well known is its ability to store food in its cheeks until it is ready to eat—just like a hamster! Sphinxes are famous for their enigmatic powers. In *The Goblet of Fire*, Harry had to answer the sphinx's riddle to proceed through the maze during the Triwizard Tournament.

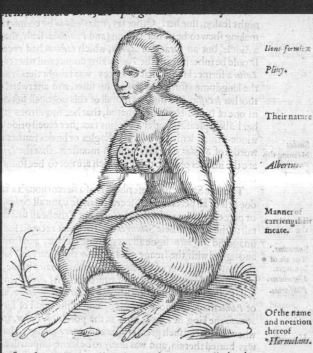

▲
EDWARD TOPSELL, *THE HISTORIE OF FOURE-FOOTED BEASTES* (LONDON, 1607)
British Library

IT HAD THE BODY OF AN OVERLARGE LION: GREAT CLAWED PAWS AND A LONG YELLOWISH TAIL ENDING IN A BROWN TUFT. ITS HEAD, HOWEVER, WAS THAT OF A WOMAN. SHE TURNED HER LONG, ALMOND-SHAPED EYES UPON HARRY AS HE APPROACHED.

—*HARRY POTTER AND THE GOBLET OF FIRE*

▲
THE RESTRICTED
SECTION
BY MARY GRANDPRÉ
Scholastic

FORBIDDEN BOOKS

The Restricted Section of the Hogwarts Library contains rare and valuable volumes as well
as books deemed inappropriate or dangerous for young witches and wizards. *Moste Potente
Potions*, *Magick Moste Evile*, and *Secrets of the Darkest Art* are just a few of the forbidden titles.
In this pastel illustration, the artist Mary GrandPré evokes the vantage point of the youngest
of wizards who are not yet tall enough to reach the most dangerous of books. Sneaking into
the Restricted Section is the very first thing Harry does with his Invisibility Cloak in *The
Sorcerer's Stone*. In the absence of a charmed cloak, students are granted access only with
a note signed by a professor; Hermione obtains the gullible Professor Lockhart's signature
when she needs to research the Polyjuice Potion in *The Chamber of Secrets*.

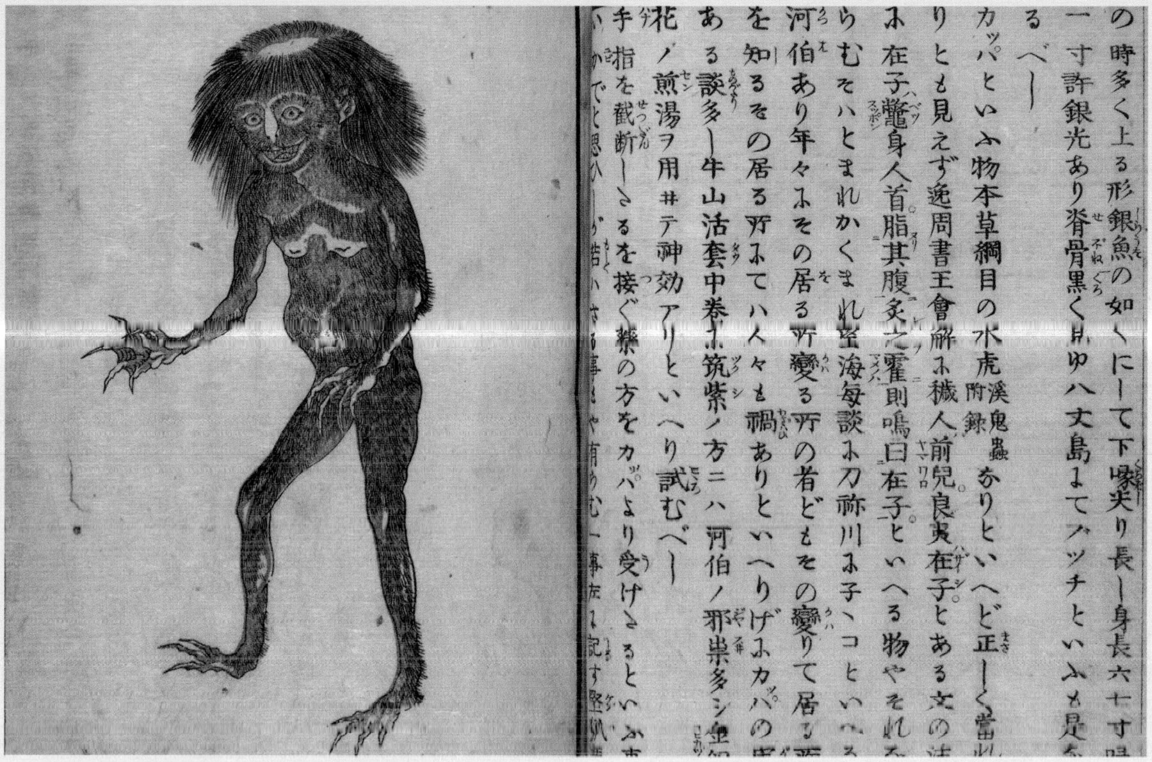

THE KAPPA

The kappa takes its name from the Japanese words for "river" and "child." These were mischievous creatures, with the power to pull people into the lakes or rivers in which they dwelt. The wizarding world's famous Magizoologist Newt Scamander recognized this danger, noting that "The Kappa feeds on human blood but may be persuaded not to harm a person if it is thrown a cucumber with that person's name carved into it." The *neneko* kappa, illustrated above, moved to a new location every year, causing destruction wherever it went.

▲ A *NENEKO KAPPA* IN
*AKAMATSU SŌTAN,
TONEGAWA ZUSHI*
(EDO, 1855)
British Library

"The kappa's head has a distinctive hollow to contain its vital fluid. In Fantastic Beasts and Where to Find Them, *Scamander advised that the wizard should trick the kappa into bowing, so that the water in its head would run out, depriving it of its strength."*
JULIAN HARRISON
Lead Curator

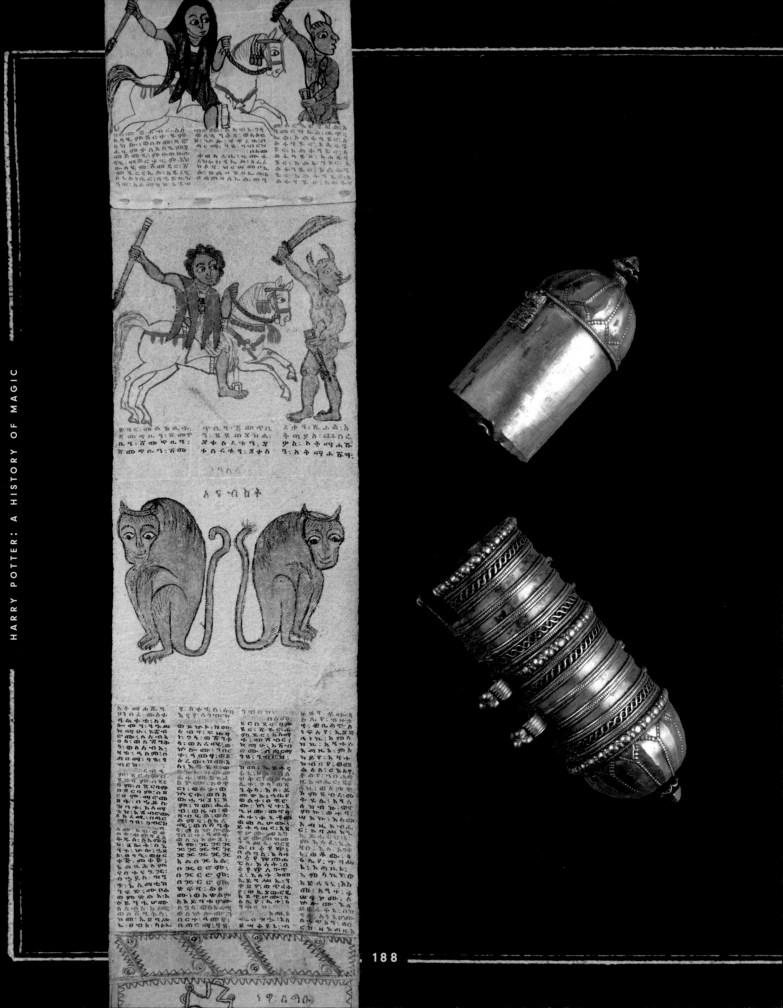

AMULET SCROLLS

Amulets, written on leather or metal, have been worn by Ethiopians and other peoples in the Horn of Africa for thousands of years. This practice remains strongest in the northern Highlands of Ethiopia, where amulets are believed to bring health, protect babies, and ward off the evil eye. The parchment scrolls themselves are known as *Ketab*, and they vary considerably in length. They are kept in leather cases, or in cylindrical silver containers like those shown here. The *Ketab* can then be hung up at home or worn around the neck, depending on their size. This particular scroll was created to protect its owner from harm. It contains prayers for undoing spells (*maftehé seray*), after which the talismanic drawings were added, giving effect to its powers.

◄ ►
**TWO AMULET SCROLLS,
ONE WITH A PROTECTIVE
CYLINDRICAL CASE
(ETHIOPIA, 18TH CENTURY)**
British Library

"The drawings in this scroll have a specific purpose. They are intended to cure sickness, to exorcise demons, and to protect those taking long and difficult journeys."

EYOB DERILLO
Curator

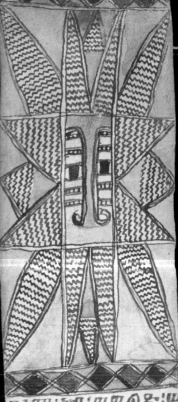

ETHIOPIAN TALISMANS

This personally annotated, magical recipe book was made in Ethiopia. Written in Ge'ez, also known as classic Ethiopic, it contains a rich collection of protective amulets, talismans, charms, and incantations. This manuscript would have belonged to an exorcist or a Däbtära, a highly educated religious figure. Däbtäras typically study for several years or come from families of clergy. On these pages are talismans and geometric images, used for making amulet scrolls, and accompanied by prayers for undoing spells and charms. Talismanic drawing focuses on the image of the eye, providing a defense against the evil eye and the dark arts.

▼ ▶

**AN ETHIOPIAN
MAGICAL RECIPE
BOOK (1750)**
British Library

"Since medieval times, Däbtäras have worked in the courts or have taught in small parish schools, supplementing their income by producing amulet scrolls and practicing traditional medicine. From the marginal notes in this recipe book, we can deduce with some certainty that it belonged to a practitioner of magic."

EYOB DERILLO
Curator

Camphur

2.

Pirassoipi.

3.
Licor
Ions.

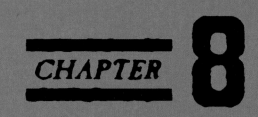

CHAPTER 8

CARE
of MAGICAL

CREATURES

HAGRID

Rubeus Hagrid, the half-giant, introduced Harry to many of the wonderful creatures that stride, scuttle, and soar around the wizarding world. Jim Kay's artwork brings to life Hagrid's mane of black hair and "wild, tangled beard." "Hagrid is a relief to draw," says Jim Kay, "because drawing children you can't put a line wrong, a misplaced scribble can age a child by ten years. There are no such problems with Hagrid; he's a mass of scribbles with eyes." In the Harry Potter books, the gamekeeper was a reliable and trustworthy presence, despite his blind spot toward dangerous beasts. Hagrid became the professor for Care of Magical Creatures in Harry's third year.

▲
PORTRAIT OF RUBEUS HAGRID BY JIM KAY
Bloomsbury

"HAGRID [IS] THE EARTHY, WARM, AND PHYSICAL MAN, LORD OF THE FOREST; DUMBLEDORE THE SPIRITUAL THEORETICIAN, BRILLIANT, IDEALIZED, AND SOMEWHAT DETACHED. EACH IS A NECESSARY COUNTERPOINT TO THE OTHER AS HARRY SEEKS FATHER FIGURES IN HIS NEW WORLD."
—J.K. ROWLING ON POTTERMORE

A GIANT FROM UNDERGROUND

Were skeletons of 300-foot-tall giants found on Mount Erice in Sicily? While traveling in Italy, the German author Athanasius Kircher became fascinated with the idea of what might lie beneath the earth. He even climbed inside the volcano Mount Vesuvius, which had last erupted seven years earlier. Kircher claimed that an enormous skeleton had been discovered sitting in a Sicilian cave in the 14th century. In Kircher's *Mundus Subterraneus* ("The Underground World") he shows the scale of it in comparison to a normal human, the Biblical giant Goliath, a Swiss giant, and a Mauritanian giant.

"Throughout history, there have been records of both dangerous and friendly giants. An example of the latter is the Cornish giant Holiburn, who died of grief after accidentally killing a youth by tapping him playfully on the head. This anecdote shows that, despite their lethal size and phenomenal strength, giants are often big of heart."

JOANNA NORLEDGE
Curator

▲
THE SKELETON OF A GIANT, IN ATHANASIUS KIRCHER, *MUNDUS SUBTERRANEUS* (AMSTERDAM, 1678)
American Museum of Natural History Library

HAGRID AND HARRY

AT GRINGOTTS

In this original drawing by J.K. Rowling, Hagrid is shown taking Harry on his first trip to his vault at Gringotts, located in the caverns deep beneath the wizarding bank. Hagrid covers his eyes with his hand during the ride. Harry, on the other hand, keeps his eyes "wide open" for the whole journey. This image shows visually Hagrid's discomfort at being cramped up inside the Gringotts cart. J.K. Rowling uses the giant's streaming hair and the torch flame bending in the wind to convey a sense of rattling speed.

▲ DRAWING OF HARRY AND HAGRID AT GRINGOTTS BY J.K. ROWLING
J.K. Rowling

[. . .] WHEN THE CART STOPPED AT LAST BESIDE A SMALL DOOR IN THE PASSAGE WALL, HAGRID GOT OUT AND HAD TO LEAN AGAINST THE WALL TO STOP HIS KNEES FROM TREMBLING.

—*HARRY POTTER AND THE SORCERER'S STONE*

A DRAFT OF *THE SORCERER'S STONE*

This typed draft represents an unedited version of *Harry Potter and the Sorcerer's Stone*. As part of the editorial process, a literary draft may be amended in order to improve the pacing. For a scene like this, full of action and drama, some passages were subsequently shortened to move the story along more quickly. Some scenes, in turn, may be completely cut, such as the encounter with a preoccupied Nearly Headless Nick, and Hermione reciting the textbook definition of trolls, both shown on page 167 of this draft.

"Hello, hello," he said absently, "Just pondering a little problem, don't take any notice of me..."

"What's Peeves done this time?" asked Harry.

"No, no, it's not Peeves I'm worried about," said Nearly Headless Nick, looking thoughtfully at Harry. "Tell me, Mr. Potter, if you were

167

worried that someone was up to something they shouldn't be, would you tell someone else, who might be able to stop it, even if you didn't think much of the person who might be able to help?"

"Er - you mean - would I go to Snape about Malfoy, for instance?"

"Something like that, something like that...."

"I don't think Snape would help me, but it'd be worth a try, I suppose," said Harry curiously.

"Yes... yes... thank you, Mr. Potter..."

Nearly Headless Nick glided away. Harry and Ron watched him go, puzzled looks on their faces.

"I suppose you're bound not to make much sense if you've been beheaded," said Ron.

Quirrell was late for class. He rushed in looking pale and anxious and told them to turn to "p-page fifty four" at once, to look at "t-t-trolls."

"N-now, who c-c-can tell me the three types of t-troll? Yes, Miss G-

167

Granger?"

"Mountain-dwelling, river-dwelling and sea-dwelling," said Hermione promptly. "Mountain-dwelling trolls are the biggest, they're pale grey, bald, have skin tougher than a rhinoceros and are stronger than ten men. However, their brains are only the size of a pea, so they're easy to confuse -"

"Very g-good, thank you, Miss Gr -"

◀ ▶
A TYPED DRAFT OF *HARRY POTTER AND THE SORCERER'S STONE* BY J.K. ROWLING
J.K. Rowling

CARE OF MAGICAL CREATURES

"River trolls are light green and have stringy hair -"

"Y-y-yes, thank you, that's excell -"

" - and sea trolls are purplish grey and -"

"Oh, someone shut her up," said Seamus loudly. A few people laughed.

There was a loud clatter as Hermione jumped to her feet, knocking her chair over, and ran out of the room with her face in her hands. A very awkward silence followed.

"Oh d-d-dear," said Professor Quirrell.

*

When Harry woke up next day, the first thing he noticed was a delicious smell in the air.

"It's pumpkin, of course!" said Ron, "Today's Hallowe'en!"

Harry soon realised that Hallowe'en at Hogwarts was a sort of mini-Christmas. When they got down to the Great Hall for breakfast, they found that it had been decorated with thousands of real bats, which were hanging off the ceiling and window-sills, fast asleep. Hagrid was putting hollow pumpkins on all the tables.

"Big feast tonight," he grinned at them, "See yeh there!"

There was a holiday feeling in the air because lessons would be finishing early. No-one was in much of a mood for work, which annoyed Professor McGonagall.

168

"Unless you settle down, you won't be going to the feast at all," she said, a few minutes into Transfiguration. She stared at them until they had all fallen silent. Then she raised her eyebrows.

"And where is Hermione Granger?"

They all looked at each other.

"Miss Patil, have you seen Miss Granger?"

Parvati shook her head.

---

cupboard doors, but not a hint of a troll did they find.

They'd just decided to try the dungeons when they heard footsteps.

"If it's Snape, he'll send us back - quick, behind here!"

They squeezed into an alcove behind a statue of Godfrey the Gormless.

Sure enough, a moment later they caught a glimpse of Snape's hook nose rushing past. Then they heard him whisper "Alohomora!" and a click.

"Where's he gone?" Ron whispered.

"No idea - quick, before he gets back -"

They dashed down the stairs, three at a time, and rushed headlong into the cold darkness of the dungeons. They passed the room where they usually had Potions and were soon walking through passages they'd never seen before. They slowed down, looking around. The walls were wet and slimey and the air was dank.

"I never realised they were so big," Harry whispered as they turned yet another corner and saw three more passageways to choose from. "It's like Gringotts down here..."

173

Ron sniffed the damp air.

"Can you smell something?"

Harry sniffed too. Ron was right. Above the generally musty smell of the dungeons was another smell, which was rapidly becoming a foul stench, a mixture of old socks and public toilets, the concrete kind that no-one seems to clean.

And then they heard it. A low grunting - heavy breathing - and the shuffling footfalls of gigantic feet.

They froze - they couldn't tell where the sound was coming from amid all the echoes -

Ron suddenly pointed; at the end of one of the passageways,

"Here you can read a slightly different account of Ron and Harry coming face-to-face with a troll in the girls' bathroom. For example, the paragraph at the top of page 175 is reduced to two sentences in the published text. This draft also preserves the idea of securing the door with a chain, rather than locking the door with a key, as occurs in the published version."

JOANNA NORLEDGE
Curator

...nething huge was moving. It hadn't seen them... it ambled out of
...ht...

"Merlin's beard," said Ron softly, "It's enormous..."

They looked at each other. Now that they had seen the troll, their ...deas of fighting it seemed a bit - stupid. But neither of them wanted to ...e the one to say this. Harry tried to look brave and unconcerned.

"Did you see if it had a club?" Trolls, he knew, often carried clubs.

Ron shook his head, also trying to look as though he wasn't ...bothered.

"You know what we should do?" said Harry, "Follow it. Try and lock it in one of the dungeons - trap it, you know..."

If Ron had been hoping Harry was going to say, "Let's go back to the feast", he didn't show it. Locking up the troll was better than trying to fight it.

"Good idea," he said.

They crept down the passageway. The stench grew stronger as they reached the end. Very slowly, they peered around the corner.

174

There it was. It was shuffling away from them. Even from the back, it was a horrible sight. Twelve feet tall, its skin was a dull, granite grey, its great lumpy body like a boulder with its small bald head perched on top like a coconut. It had short legs thick as tree trunks with flat, horny feet. The smell coming from it was incredible. It was holding a huge wooden club, which dragged along the floor because its arms were so long.

They pulled their heads back out of sight.

"Did you see the size of that club?" Ron whispered. Neither of them could have lifted it.

"We'll wait for it to go into one of the chambers and then barricade the door," said Harry. He looked back around the corner.

The troll had stopped next to a doorway and was peering inside. Harry could see its face now; it had tiny red eyes, a great squashed nose and a gaping mouth. It also had long, dangling ears which waggled as it shook its head, making up its tiny mind where to go next. Then it slouched slowly into the chamber.

Harry looked around, searching -

"There!" he whispered to Ron, "See? On the wall there!"

A long, rusty chain was suspended about half way down the passageway. Harry and Ron darted forward and pulled it off its nail. Trying to stop it clinking, they tiptoed towards the open door, praying the troll wasn't about to come out of it -

Harry seized the door handle and pulled it shut: with trembling hands, they looped the chain around the handle, hooked it onto a bolt sticking out of the wall and pulled it tight.

"It'll take it a while to get out of that," Harry panted, as they pulled the chain back across the door and tied it firmly to a torch bracket, "Come

175

on, let's go and tell them we've caught it!"

Flushed with their victory they started to run back up the passage, but as they reached the corner they heard something that made their hearts stop - a high, petrified scream - and it was coming from the chamber they'd just chained up -

"Oh, no," said Ron, pale as the Bloody Baron.

"There's someone in there!" Harry gasped.

"Hermione!" they said together.

It was the last thing they wanted to do, but what choice did they have? Wheeling around they sprinted back to the door and ripped the chain off, fumbling in their panic - Harry pulled the door open - they ran inside.

◀ DRAWING OF
A MOUNTAIN
TROLL BY
JIM KAY
Bloomsbury

▶ TROLL
BY MARY
GRANDPRÉ
Scholastic

A MOUNTAIN TROLL

This is a preparatory study of a mountain troll or, to use the scientific name, *Troglodytarum alpinum*. In J.K. Rowling's wizarding world trolls can grow to twelve feet tall, and are extremely strong and thick skinned. Due to the very small size of their brains, they are easily confused and quick to flare into a temper. A violent disposition, alongside a taste for human flesh, meant that these creatures were classed as dangerous by the Ministry of Magic. This troll, covered in growths and with a perplexed look in its eye, is typical of its species.

IT WAS A HORRIBLE SIGHT. TWELVE FEET TALL, ITS SKIN WAS A DULL, GRANITE GRAY, ITS GREAT LUMPY BODY LIKE A BOULDER WITH ITS SMALL BALD HEAD PERCHED ON TOP LIKE A COCONUT. IT HAD SHORT LEGS THICK AS TREE TRUNKS WITH FLAT, HORNY FEET.

—*HARRY POTTER AND THE SORCERER'S STONE*

▶
**DRAWING
OF NEARLY
HEADLESS
NICK BY J.K.
ROWLING
(1991)**
J.K. Rowling

NEARLY HEADLESS
NICK

NEARLY HEADLESS NICK

J.K. Rowling's drawing of Nearly Headless Nick shows the Gryffindor ghost demonstrating exactly how you can be *nearly* headless. As a ghost, Nick could not enjoy simple pleasures such as eating food, a fact that he lamented at Harry's first Hogwarts feast. He also nursed resentment at his botched beheading, which prevented him from joining the Headless Hunt. J.K. Rowling has elsewhere defined a ghost in Harry Potter's world as, "the transparent, three-dimensional imprint of a deceased witch or wizard, which continues to exist in the mortal world."

▶
DRAWING
OF PEEVES
BY J.K.
ROWLING
(1991)
J.K. Rowling

PEEVES THE
POLTERGEIST

PEEVES THE POLTERGEIST

Peeves is shown here in his visible form, but he was able to become invisible at will. A poltergeist (meaning "noisy ghost" in German) is generally understood to be a malevolent spirit. In this drawing, Peeves almost resembles a court jester, with his curly-toed shoes, bow tie, and spotted hat. J.K. Rowling has captured his glinting, wicked eyes, emphasizing them with a pair of slanted eyebrows. The poltergeist's pranks were often crude, but extremely effective. Following Professor Umbridge, then blowing raspberries whenever she spoke, is a prime and very Peeve-ish example.

THE ESCAPE FROM

GRINGOTTS

This is the very first handwritten draft of the scene in *Harry Potter and the Deathly Hallows* in which Harry, Ron, and Hermione escape from Gringotts bank on the back of a dragon. The first page describes the dramatic escape, and a little arrow in the corner indicates that the scene continues on the previous page. There are many crossings-out and added sentences in both margins. The page on the right-hand side describes Harry destroying a cup, the Hufflepuff Horcrux, while his friends are still in the Lestranges' vault. This is an event that does not take place in the published text—instead Hermione is the one who destroys the cup.

"When I'm planning I often have multiple ideas popping up at the same time, so I'm attempting to catch the best ones as they fly by and preserve them on paper. My notebooks are full of arrows and triple asterisks instructing me to move forward four pages, past the ideas I jotted down hurriedly twenty minutes ago, to continue the thread of the story."

J.K. ROWLING

"This manuscript demonstrates that J.K. Rowling did not necessarily write the scenes in her books in order, and that some of them were later rewritten. Note how Harry's dialogue is represented by an X on the second page, to be filled in with something appropriate at a later stage."

JOANNA NORLEDGE
Curator

sword ~~and~~ seized Griphook's hand and pulled. The blistered, howling Goblin emerged by degrees.

~~'Hermione let me down!' Harry yelled,~~

'X' yelled Harry and he landed on the bumpy surface of the ~~Dr~~ swelling ~~treasure~~ under the goblin on ~~cup~~ ~~his shoulder~~ again, ~~but~~ now ~~all~~ ~~crowd~~ ~~them~~ ~~were~~ a hundred swords of Gryffindor ~~multiplying~~ were multiplying all around him.

'The real one—' he groaned: ~~to~~ ~~he~~ ~~they~~ had to destroy the Horcrux, ~~to~~ 'where its got the cup on 'it—'

~~And then it was~~

The jewelled hilt was ~~showed~~ into his hand. ~~Griphook~~ ~~had~~ spotted and seized it. In one fluid action, ~~he~~ ~~then~~ the ~~air~~ hot was full of ~~too~~ ~~yet~~ screams, ~~and~~ ~~it~~ Harry ~~gave~~ ~~too~~ ~~raised~~ the sword into the air flew the cup ~~high~~ up, turned over and fell, and he impaled it on the blade ~~on~~ ~~its~~ ~~descent,~~ ~~so~~ ~~that~~ the point of the sword penetrating the bottom of the cup.

~~There was a~~

He heard no sound, but a bloodlike liquid gushed from the punctured cup, splashing over ~~all~~ ~~of~~ ~~them~~, Hermione who choked and gasped, and then they were ~~sliding~~ uncontrollably out of the vault on a great mass of gold and silver: the waiting goblins had reopened the door ~~again~~.

~~The treasure~~ in his head

~~Harry~~ ~~had~~ only one thought: goblins did not carry wands.

"Aldrovandi's study provides detailed descriptions of snakes, dragons, and other monsters, explaining their temperament and habitat. Depicted here are two types of Ethiopian dragon, distinguishable by the ridges on their back."

ALEXANDER LOCK
Curator

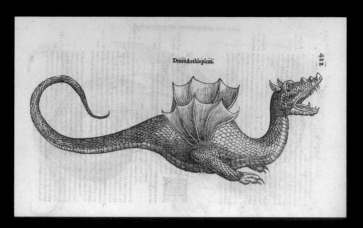

▶

ULISSE ALDROVANDI, SERPENTUM ET DRACONUM HISTORIAE (BOLOGNA, 1640)
British Library

ETHIOPIAN DRAGONS

On May 13, 1572, the same day that Pope Gregory XIII was invested, a "monstrous dragon" was found in the countryside near Bologna. Recognized as a bad omen, the dragon's body was sent for analysis to the Pope's cousin, the celebrated naturalist and collector Ulisse Aldrovandi. Although Aldrovandi quickly wrote up his findings, his work was not published for nearly 60 years, appearing posthumously in 1640 as *A History of Snakes and Dragons*. This might have been just the sort of text Hagrid needed when "looking up stuff about dragons" for hatching Norbert, or when Harry was in the library pulling down "every book he could find on dragons" for the Triwizard Tournament.

PROBABLY THE MOST FAMOUS OF ALL MAGICAL BEASTS, DRAGONS ARE AMONG THE MOST DIFFICULT TO HIDE. THE FEMALE IS GENERALLY LARGER AND MORE AGGRESSIVE THAN THE MALE, THOUGH NEITHER SHOULD BE APPROACHED BY ANY BUT HIGHLY SKILLED AND TRAINED WIZARDS.

—*FANTASTIC BEASTS AND WHERE TO FIND THEM*

DRAGON EGGS

Jim Kay's study of dragon eggs reflects the sheer variety of dragon species in Harry Potter's world. The artist painted the shape and base colors of the eggs first, then added and overlaid extra details and flecks of color to the final versions. A scale to indicate the size of these eggs shows the smallest to be about six inches high (about the same size as an ostrich egg) and the largest up to fifteen inches. Some of the eggs are simple and almost ordinary looking, while others unmistakably belong in the magical world. All of the egg species would have been familiar, of course, to Newt Scamander.

◄
**DRAGON EGGS
BY JIM KAY**
Bloomsbury

AN OUTSTANDING OWL

First year students at Hogwarts were allowed to bring an owl, cat, or a toad to school—each animal had an historic magical significance as a powerful familiar of witches and wizards. In *The Sorcerer's Stone*, Hagrid bought Harry a beautiful female Snowy Owl, whom the boy named Hedwig. John James Audubon's iconic watercolor contains a pair of these enormous birds. In front is the larger female—26 inches tall with a wingspan of 56 inches— with salt-and-pepper plumage, while the smaller male gets paler with age. Audubon's dazzling watercolor is his model for a plate in *The Birds of America* (1827 – 38), which was engraved by Robert Havell Jr. The artist, who was the first person to portray all his birds life-size, painted the pair on double-elephant-size paper (40 inches high). The owl's hypnotic eyes—with yellow irises designed to gather maximum light in the polar twilight—are riveted on the beholder. Audubon knew that visually stunning Snowy Owls hunt during the day or early evening rather than at night. To make these majestic creatures stand out from the white paper, he created a dusky background with a gathering winter storm.

▶

JOHN JAMES AUDUBON, *SNOWY OWL (BUBO SCANDIACUS)*, *WATERCOLOR STUDY FOR HAVELL PL. 121* (UNITED STATES, 1829)
New-York Historical Society

①

②

DAWN OF ORNITHOLOGY

These extraordinary "portraits" of owls reflect the
humanistic culture of 16th century Europe that
emphasized learning through observation and the quest
for knowledge. They document one of the most complex,
early scientific efforts to catalog natural phenomena
taxonomically. At the dawn of ornithology, 16th century
artists aspired to portray their birds life-size, but the

③

④

① ISAAC LA GRESE (ATTRIBUTED),
BARN OWL (TYTO ALBA),
DARK-BREASTED VARIANT,
EFFRAIE DES CLOCHERS
(FRANCE OR SWITZERLAND,
CA. 1548–55)
New-York Historical Society

② PIERRE VASE/ESKRICH (ATTRIBUTED),
EUROASIAN SCOPS OWL (OTUS
SCOPS), RUFOUS VARIANT, PETIT-DUC
SCOPS, (FRANCE OR SWITZERLAND,
CA. 1548–55)
New-York Historical Society

③ UNIDENTIFIED ARTIST
ASSOCIATED WITH CONRAD
GESNER, *GESNER'S "NOCTUA"*
(FRANCE OR SWITZERLAND,
CA. 1554)
New-York Historical Society

④ UNIDENTIFIED AVIAN ARTIST,
EAGLE OWL (BUBO BUBO),
GRAND-DUC D'EUROPE (FRANCE
OR SWITZERLAND, CA. 1548–55)
New-York Historical Society

A CUNNING CAT

Conrad Gessner was a Swiss naturalist whose *Historiae Animalium* is one of the earliest printed zoological texts. Gessner used realistic woodcuts to illustrate the animals being described, including enough detail to aid identification, unlike the earlier fable and bestiary collections. Cats already had a bad reputation—here they are said to possess "a cunning character." Edward Topsell, the first English translator of Gessner's work, noted, "The familiars of witches do most ordinarily appear in the shape of cats, which is an argument that the beast is dangerous to soul and body." Elsewhere, Gessner asserted that, "men have been known to lose their strength, perspire violently, and even faint at the sight of a cat."

▲
CONRAD GESSNER,
HISTORIAE ANIMALIUM
(ZÜRICH, 1551–87)
British Library

SOMETHING BRUSHED HIS ANKLES. HE LOOKED DOWN AND SAW THE CARETAKER'S SKELETAL GRAY CAT, MRS. NORRIS, SLINKING PAST HIM. SHE TURNED LAMPLIKE YELLOW EYES ON HIM FOR A MOMENT BEFORE DISAPPEARING BEHIND A STATUE OF WILFRED THE WISTFUL.

—*HARRY POTTER AND THE ORDER OF THE PHOENIX*

AT LONG LAST, THE TRAIN STOPPED AT HOGSMEADE STATION, AND THERE WAS A GREAT SCRAMBLE TO GET OUTSIDE; OWLS HOOTED, CATS MEOWED, AND NEVILLE'S PET TOAD CROAKED LOUDLY FROM UNDER HIS HAT.

—*HARRY POTTER AND THE PRISONER OF AZKABAN*

▲
J.B. VON SPIX, *ANIMALIA NOVA, SIVE SPECIES NOVÆ TESTUDINUM ET RANARUM, QUAS IN ITINERE PER BRASILIAM ANNIS 1817–1820 . . . COLLEGIT, ET DESCRIPSIT* (MUNICH, 1824)
British Library

"Toads often feature in old folk remedies for common ailments and complaints. Rubbing a toad on a wart was said to cure it, but only if you impaled the toad and left it to die."

JOANNA NORLEDGE
Curator

A TOXIC TOAD

Toads have long featured in magical folklore, their properties ranging from predicting the weather to bringing good luck. When Johann Baptist von Spix, the German biologist, visited Brazil he described this species of toad, *Bufo agua*, also known as the cane toad or giant marine toad. The cane is the world's largest toad, recognizable for its unwebbed hands and feet, its brown-colored iris, and the venom glands dotted across the surface of its skin, which produce a toxic, milky secretion. Unfortunately, it is dangerous to many animals, such as dogs. At Hogwarts, Neville Longbottom's pet toad Trevor seemed much more benign.

[...] A SPIDER THE SIZE OF A SMALL ELEPHANT EMERGED, VERY SLOWLY. THERE WAS GRAY IN THE BLACK OF HIS BODY AND LEGS, AND EACH OF THE EYES ON HIS UGLY, PINCERED HEAD WAS MILKY WHITE.

—HARRY POTTER AND THE CHAMBER OF SECRETS

RON AND HARRY
MEET ARAGOG

Imagine, if your greatest fear were spiders, how you might feel meeting an Acromantula. Jim Kay's image of the horrific spider captures every creepy detail of the carnivorous creature that Harry and Ron encountered in the Forbidden Forest. In the background, hundreds of spiders' legs become indistinguishable from the spiky trees around them. Strands of cobwebs gleam white in Harry's wandlight. Aragog is the originator of this spider colony—a combination of too many eyes and too many horribly hairy legs. This painting was layered with a watercolor tone and edited to create the final image.

▶
ARAGOG BY JIM KAY
Bloomsbury

BIRD-EATING SPIDERS

Maria Sibylla Merian was a pioneering naturalist and zoological illustrator, celebrated for her groundbreaking work on South American insects. Between 1699 and 1701, Merian worked in the Dutch colony of Surinam, where she made the drawings of these arachnids for *Metamorphosis insectorum Surinamensium*. Merian's scientific expedition to this remote location was reputedly the first to be led by a European woman. Like Hagrid, who cared for Aragog when he "was only a boy," Merian's fascination with insects developed in childhood. Many of the species first encountered by Merian in Surinam were unknown to Western science.

"When Merian published this image of giant, bird-eating spiders, she was denounced as a fantasist by her male peers. Her hand-painted books nevertheless sold well, but it was not until 1863 that the genuine existence of this bird-eating spider was finally accepted."

ALEXANDER LOCK
Curator

◄
MARIA SIBYLLA MERIAN,
METAMORPHOSIS INSECTORUM SURINAMENSIUM
(AMSTERDAM, 1705)
American Museum of Natural History Library

BUCKBEAK THE HIPPOGRIFF

In this Jim Kay illustration, Buckbeak has taken over his beloved owner's bed, a snack of dead ferrets resting under his claws. Hagrid received orders from the Ministry of Magic to tether the hippogriff, but he could not bear to leave "Beaky" tied up outside, alone in the snow. The interior of Hagrid's cabin was drawn from the real-life gardener's hut at Calke Abbey in Derbyshire, England. The vibrant blue highlights echo the famous bluebells that grow there. The word "hippogriff" is derived from the ancient Greek for "horse" and the Italian for "griffin." The griffin, with its eagle's head and lion's hindquarters, is said to be the hippogriff's ancestor.

▶

**BUCKBEAK
THE
HIPPOGRIFF
BY JIM KAY**
Bloomsbury

ORLANDO FURIOSO

Ludovico Ariosto was the first to describe the hippogriff in 1516 in his epic poem *Orlando Furioso*. He was inspired by the Roman author Virgil, who used the union of a horse with a griffin as a metaphor for ill-fated love—a central theme in *Orlando Furioso*. In this 18th-century illustration, the knight, Ruggiero, has tied his hippogriff mount to a tree. Unbeknownst to him, the tree was actually another knight who had been transformed by an evil sorceress. Her monstrous minions can be seen approaching in the background.

CANTO. VI.

"This luxury edition of Orlando Furioso *was printed on vellum (calf skin) with engravings after Pietro Antonio Novelli. It once belonged to King George III."*
ALEXANDER LOCK
Curator

◄
**LUDOVICO ARIOSTO,
ORLANDO FURIOSO
(VENICE, 1772–3)**
British Library

THE UNICORN IS A BEAUTIFUL BEAST FOUND THROUGHOUT THE FORESTS OF NORTHERN EUROPE. IT IS A PURE WHITE, HORNED HORSE WHEN FULLY GROWN, THOUGH THE FOALS ARE INITIALLY GOLDEN AND TURN SILVER BEFORE ACHIEVING MATURITY.

—*FANTASTIC BEASTS AND WHERE TO FIND THEM*

HUNTING THE UNICORN

Ever since the Greek physician Ctesias first described the medicinal properties of unicorns around 400 B.C.E., these elusive animals have attracted human hunters. This image of the killing and skinning of the "pirassoipi," a twin-horned unicorn, is found in a study by Ambroise Paré, surgeon to the French Crown. Unsurprisingly, the hunters in the scene have a cruel appearance. As Firenze told Harry in *The Sorcerer's Stone*, "it is a monstrous thing, to slay a unicorn."

▶

AMBROISE PARÉ, *DISCOURS D'AMBROISE PARÉ, CONSEILLER, ET PREMIER CHIRURGIEN DU ROY. ASÇAVOIR, DE LA MUMIE, DE LA LICORNE, DES VENINS, ET DE LA PESTE* (PARIS, 1582)
British Library

DE LA LICORNE.

FIGVRE DV PIRASSOIPI, ESPECE DE
Licorne d'Italie.

27

grow a spiral tusk—actually an elongated tooth—up to ten feet long. When marketed as unicorn horn, the tusks could command very high prices and were collected by royalty across Europe. This impressive specimen was acquired by Arctic explorer John Stanwell-Fletcher in the first half of the 20th century and given to the Explorers Club in New York City.

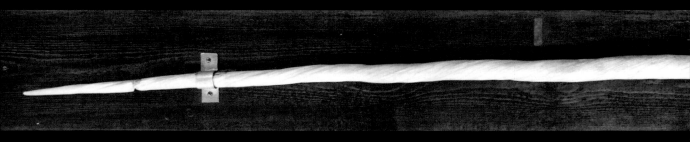

▲
NARWHAL TUSK
The Explorers Club, New York City

"HARRY POTTER, DO YOU KNOW WHAT UNICORN BLOOD IS USED FOR?"

"NO," SAID HARRY, STARTLED BY THE ODD QUESTION. "WE'VE ONLY USED THE HORN AND TAIL-HAIR IN POTIONS."

—*HARRY POTTER AND THE SORCERER'S STONE*

des Drogues, Livre Premier. 9

CHAPITRE II.
De la Licorne.

Camphur

1.

2.

Pirassoipi.

3.
Licornes de
Jonstonius

FIVE SPECIES OF UNICORN

The *Histoire générale des Drogues* was a practical manual that described an array of popular 17th-century medicinal ingredients. It was written by Pierre Pomet, a Parisian pharmacist and chief apothecary to King Louis XIV of France. In the chapter on the unicorn, Pomet would not confirm the animal's existence, conceding that "we know not the real truth of the matter," but he did acknowledge that what was commonly sold as unicorn's horn "is the horn of a certain fish called narwhal." According to Pomet, whatever its origin, the horn was "well used, on account of the great properties attributed to it, principally against poisons."

"Accompanying Pomet's text are the images of five different species of unicorn. These are the camphur (a horned ass from Arabia), the pirassoipi (a unicorn with twin horns), and three unidentified breeds noted by the naturalist John Johnstone in 1632."

ALEXANDER LOCK
Curator

▲
PIERRE POMET, HISTOIRE GÉNÉRALE DES DROGUES, TRAITANT DES PLANTES, DES ANIMAUX ET DES MINÉRAUX (PARIS, 1694)
British Library

A LION-LIKE UNICORN

This unusual unicorn appears in a 16th-century Greek manuscript. The accompanying text is a poem about the natural world composed by the Byzantine poet Manuel Philes. According to the poem, the unicorn was a wild beast with a dangerous bite—it had the tail of a boar and the mouth of a lion. If such a unicorn was encountered, the beast could only be snared by a woman. This is in line with medieval folklore stipulating that unicorns must be captured by female virgins. The unicorn would place its head in the virgin's lap and then fall asleep, allowing the hunter to sneak up on it unawares.

► **MANUEL PHILES, *ON THE PROPERTIES OF ANIMALS* (PARIS, 16TH CENTURY)** *British Library*

*"Jim Kay's delicate study of the
single phoenix feather shows how
the different colors blend, in a
similar way to that of less exotic
birds such as the mallard."*

JOANNA NORLEDGE
Curator

FAWKES THE PHOENIX

Harry Potter first met Fawkes the phoenix in
Dumbledore's office in his second year. It happened
to be a "Burning Day," meaning that the bird burst
into flames and was reborn from the ashes before
Harry's very eyes. Later, the fully grown Fawkes came
to Harry's rescue in the Chamber of Secrets. Jim Kay's
glorious painting of the bird captures the brilliant reds
and golds of the phoenix's feathers. The image seems
to soar across the surface of the page, almost taking
off at the edges. Kay has also painted details of the
feathers, the egg, and the eye, which were used in the
final composite image.

RISING FROM THE FLAMES

This 13th-century bestiary describes and illustrates the phoenix in wonderful detail. The bird's most remarkable attribute is its ability to resurrect itself in old age. It creates its own funeral pyre from branches and plants, before fanning the flames with its wings, in order to be consumed by the fire. After the ninth day, it rises again from the ashes. This legendary ability has often been compared to the self-sacrifice and resurrection of Christ—in some traditions, the phoenix signifies the eternal life of the faithful Christian.

"The phoenix is a semi-mythical bird, seldom spotted and, according to Newt Scamander, rarely domesticated by wizards. This bestiary claims that the phoenix dwells in Arabia, but Newt Scamander extended its distribution to Egypt, India, and China."

JULIAN HARRISON
Lead Curator

▲
THE PHOENIX IN A MEDIEVAL
BESTIARY (ENGLAND, 13TH CENTURY)
British Library

THE BIRD, MEANWHILE, HAD BECOME A FIREBALL; IT GAVE ONE LOUD SHRIEK AND NEXT SECOND THERE WAS NOTHING BUT A SMOLDERING PILE OF ASH ON THE FLOOR.

—*HARRY POTTER AND THE CHAMBER OF SECRETS*

THE HISTORY AND
DESCRIPTION
OF THE PHOENIX

In 1550, when global exploration was in its infancy and new animals were being constantly discovered, the French author Guy de la Garde devoted an entire study to the phoenix. This fine volume features a hand-colored picture of the creature emerging from a burning tree. The translated caption reads: "A description of the phoenix and its fortunate place of residence, of its long life, pure conversation, excellent beauty, diverse colors, and of its end and remarkable resurrection." De la Garde dedicated the book to Princess Marguerite, a patron of the arts and sister of King Henri II of France, probably in an attempt to gain her favor through association with this miraculous bird.

"*Phoenixes are historically associated with the Sun. The crest of seven feathers on the bird's head corresponds to the seven rays which traditionally emit from the head of Helios, the Greek god of the Sun.*"
TANYA KIRK
Curator

▲ A PHOENIX, IN GUY DE
LA GARDE, *L'HISTOIRE ET
DESCRIPTION DU PHOENIX*
(PARIS, 1550)
British Library

THE SIMURGH, AN IRANIAN THUNDERBIRD

Like the phoenix or the thunderbird, its North American relative, the Iranian simurgh's exact form and qualities are much disputed. It was traditionally portrayed in pre-Islamic Iran as a composite creature with a snarling canine head, forward-pointing ears, wings, and a "peacock" tail. In Persian literature, however, the simurgh was usually depicted in flight with fantastic swirling tail feathers. It is best known in this culture as the bird who reared the hero Zal on a mountaintop and healed the wounded warrior Rustam. Subsequently, as king of the birds, the simurgh became a metaphor for God in Sufi mysticism.

"This bestiary was especially popular in Central Asia. In it the author describes the simurgh as strong enough to easily carry off an elephant. It is said to lay an egg once every three hundred years."

URSULA SIMS-WILLIAMS
Curator

▲
MAJMA' AL-GHARA'IB
"COLLECTION OF RARITIES,"
BY SULTAN MUHAMMAD BALKHI (INDIA, 1698)
British Library

A CAPTURED MERMAID

As a bookdealer, apothecary, and spy, Louis Renard could have very well kept shop in Diagon Alley. In 1719 Renard published the world's first book illustrated in full color on fishes from the waters of the East Indies. Renard featured the artwork of Samuel Fallours, a soldier residing on the Indonesian Island of Ambon. The book included hand-colored engravings of over 400 exotic fishes and 41 crustaceans, along with 2 stick insects, a dugong, and a mermaid. Despite the inclusion of affidavits attesting to the accuracy of the specimens, the scientific credibility of the work quickly came under scrutiny. Fallours's artistic license can best be seen at work in the depiction and description of a mermaid supposedly caught on the coast of Borné. Measuring 59 inches in length, she reputedly lived in a tank of water for 4 days and 7 hours and occasionally cried like a mouse. According to Renard she refused to eat despite being offered small fishes.

THE MERPEOPLE HAD GRAYISH SKIN AND LONG, WILD, DARK GREEN HAIR. THEIR EYES WERE YELLOW, AS WERE THEIR BROKEN TEETH, AND THEY WORE THICK ROPES OF PEBBLES AROUND THEIR NECKS.

—*HARRY POTTER AND THE GOBLET OF FIRE*

▶

IMAGE OF A MERMAID, IN LOUIS RENARD, *POISSONS, ÉCREVISSES ET CRABES* (AMSTERDAM, 1754)
American Museum of Natural History Library

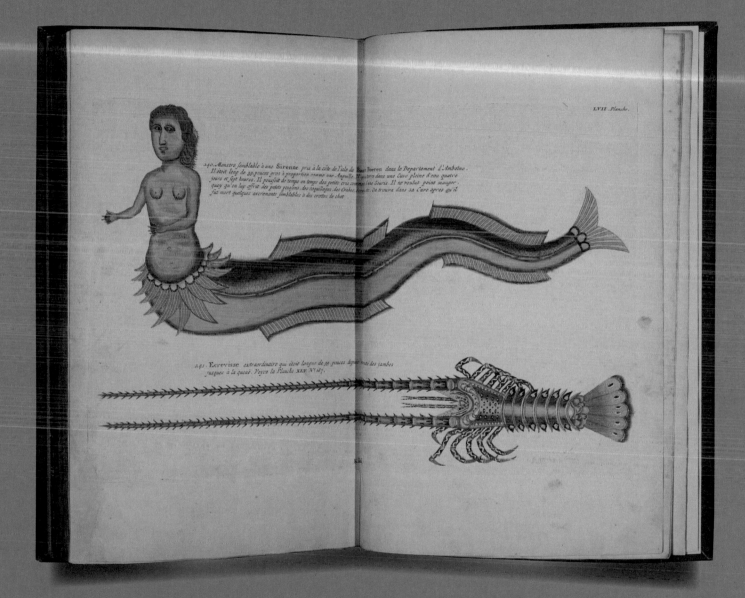

240. Monstre semblable à une Sirenne pris à la côte de l'isle de Boero Boeren dans le Departement d'Amboine. Il étoit long de 59 pouces gros à proportion comme une Anguille. Il vecut dans une Cuve pleine d'eau quatre jours et sept heures. Il poussoit de temps en temps des petits cris comme une Souris. Il ne voulut point manger, quoy qu'on luy offrit des petits poissons des coquillages des Crabes, etc.tc. On trouva dans sa Cuve apres qu'il fut mort quelques excrements semblables à des crottes de chat.

241. Ecrevisse extraordinaire qui étoit longue de 38 pouces depuis bout des jambes jusques à la queuë. Voyez la Planche XLV. N.° 187.

▲
A MERMAN (JAPAN, 19TH CENTURY)
Horniman Museum and Gardens

A REAL MERMAN?

This merman specimen looks very different from the stereotypical images familiar to us today. It is an example of *ningyo*, a Japanese supernatural creature of a type that had been displayed in Shinto shrines for hundreds of years, but was unknown outside Japan until the nineteenth century. In 1842, showman P.T. Barnum began exhibiting a mermaid specimen not unlike this one, and it caused a sensation. Barnum's mermaid is now lost, but in the second half of the nineteenth century many more of these creatures appeared in collections in Europe and North America. This example, now kept at the Horniman Museum in London, is one of several formerly owned by the great British collector Sir Henry Wellcome, who amassed over a million objects over the course of his lifetime. Unfortunately, this particular merman is not real. Extensive scientific testing has revealed it to be made of various fish parts—such as the tail from a carp, and the teeth of a wrasse—bound together with wood, metal, cloth, and papier-mâché.

"WAS THAT A
MERMAID?"

This deleted scene from *Harry Potter and the Chamber of Secrets* shows Harry and Ron crashing their enchanted Ford Anglia into the lake at Hogwarts instead of the Whomping Willow. In this version of the story, the boys are saved by the merpeople, who flip the car over and drag it to the safety of the bank. The first mermaid that Harry saw had a lower body that was "a great, scaly fishtail the colour of gun-metal." We are told that the creature's eyes, "flashing in the headlights, looked dark and threatening." At the top of page 64, the editor has written a note questioning this scene, perhaps prompting the rewriting of the chapter.

▶

THE DELETED MERPEOPLE SCENE BY J.K. ROWLING, FROM *HARRY POTTER AND THE CHAMBER OF SECRETS*
Bloomsbury

"In this draft chapter, one of the mermaids speaks to Harry and Ron in English, above the surface of the water. This contrasts with the later published texts in which merpeople can only speak Mermish above water."

JOANNA NORLEDGE
Curator

Harry thought happily of ice cold drinks in the best gold goblets, and platters piled high with delicious Hogwarts food. They flew over the edge of the great lake now, the castle right ahead of them.

"Why're you slowing down?" said Harry.

"I'm not," said Ron, stamping on the accelerator, "I don't understand -"

The car was definitely slowing. Now they were going at a walking pace.

"What's wrong with it?" said Ron, frowning at the dashboard, "Why isn't it -"

"Ron," said Harry suddenly, pointing at a dial beside the steering wheel, "We're out of petrol."

"What's petrol?" said Ron.

"It's what you need to make a car go," said Harry, irritably.

"Well, why didn't you say so before?" said Ron, as the car began to shudder alarmingly.

"I didn't know a bewitched car would need it," said Harry, grabbing the edges of his seat as the car began to vibrate madly on the spot.

"Oh no," said Ron weakly, his knuckles white on the steering wheel, "If the engine cuts out -"

The words were barely out of his mouth when the engine spluttered and died -

"NOOOOOOO!" Ron yelled.

The car dropped like a boulder; they hit the glassy surface of the lake with a deafening smash; Harry was thrown against a window, Hedwig was screaming again, Ron's foot hit Harry in the mouth; icy water was pouring in from somewhere and the car sank, slowly and steadily through the blackness. Scabbers ran across Harry's face. Water was sloshing about inside. Harry seemed to be sitting on the ceiling of the car.

"Harry?" came Ron's voice again through the dark.

"What?"

"How come we're not dead?"

HARRY POTTER: A HISTORY OF MAGIC

64

I wondered whether the mer-people scene actually works?
After all, we don't see them again... What if,
as an alternative, the car suddenly develops underwater
boosters or something - and suddenly shoots out of the water? Might
help? Too?

..."Oh, well - a fish -" said Harry, "A fish isn't going to do anything to us... I thought

it might be the giant squid."

There was a pause in which Harry wished he hadn't thought about the giant squid.

"There's loads of them," said Ron, swivelling round and gazing out of the rear

window.

Harry felt as though tiny spiders were crawling up his spine. Large dark shadows

were circling the car.

"If it's just fish..." he repeated.

And then, into the light, swam something Harry had never expected to see as long

as he lived.

It was a woman. A cloud of blackest hair, thick and tangled like seaweed, floated
all around her. Her lower body was a great, scaly fishtail the colour of gun-metal; ropes
of shells and pebbles hung about her neck, her skin was a pale, silvery grey and her eyes,
flashing in the headlights, looked dark and threatening. She gave a powerful flick of her

tail and sped into the darkness.

"Was that a *mermaid?*" said Harry.

"Well, it wasn't the giant squid," said Ron.

There was a crunching noise and the car suddenly shifted.

Harry scrambled about to press his face against the back window. About ten

merpeople, bearded men as well as long haired women, were straining against the car,

their tails swishing behind them.

"Where are they going to take us?" said Ron, pannicking.

The mermaid they had seen first rapped on the window next to Harry and made a

circular motion with her silvery hand.

"I think they're going to flip us over," said Harry quickly, "Hold on -"

"The windows have shut themselves..."

"Dad must've added safety spells..."

"Are you hurt?"

"Something's bleeding, but I think I'm OK. Are you all right?"

Harry felt the back of his head. "I've got a lump like an egg but nothing feels
broken."

"How're we going to get out of this?"

"Dunno..."

There was a jolt and an ominous silence. The roof of the car had hit the bottom of
the lake.

"Well, we can still breathe," said Ron, "But I don't know how long that's going to
..."

"Will anyone know we're here?"

"I don't know - you can't see the lake from the train station, can you?"

"Maybe someone from Hogwarts was looking out of the window."

"Yeah, maybe," said Ron bravely.

The headlights were still working. They could see a few feet of murky water and
rocks on the floor of the lake. Neither of them spoke for a while.

"We'll have to thank your Dad if we - when we get out," said Harry eventually,
"im his safety spells worked."

"Yeah... Harry..." Ron's voice was trembling, "Did you see something move out

Harry stared out at the water illuminated by the headlights. There was nothing
ut a few specks of sand were swirling as though it had been disturbed.

"What did you think you saw?" Harry asked. It was hard to keep your voice calm
concerned when your mouth was so dry.

"It looked like an enormous fish-tail," whispered Ron.

65

They grabbed the door hands and slowly, as the mer-people pushed and strained,
the car turned right over onto its wheels, clouds of silt fogging the water. Hedwig was
beating her wings furiously against the bars of her cage again.

The mer-people were now binding thick, slimy ropes of lakeweed around the car
and tying the ends around their own waists. Then, with Harry and Ron sitting in the front
seats hardly daring to breathe, they pulled... the car was lifted off the bottom and rose,
towed by the mer-people, to the surface.

"*Yes!*" said Ron, as they saw the starry sky again through their drenched windows.

The mer-people in front looked like seals, their sleek heads just visible as they
towed the car towards the bank. A few feet from the grassy bank, they felt the wheels
touch the pebbly ground of the lake again. The mer-people sank out of sight. Then the
first mermaid bobbed up at Harry's window and rapped on it. He unwound it quickly.

"We can take you no further," she said. She had a strange voice, it was both
screechy and hoarse. "The rocks are sharp in the shallows, but legs are not so easily torn
as fins..."

"No," said Harry, nervously, "Look, we can't thank you enough..."

The mermaid gave a little flick of her tail and was gone.

"Come on, I need food..." said Ron, who was shivering.

They opened the doors of the car with difficulty, picked up Hedwig and Scabbers,
braced themselves and jumped down into the freezing water, which came up above Harry's
thighs. They waded to the bank and climbed out.

"Not as pretty as they look in books, are they, mermaids?" said Ron, trying to
wring out his jeans. "Of course, they were lake people... maybe in a warm sea..."

Harry didn't answer; he was having trouble with Hedwig, who had clearly had
enough of wizard transport. He let her out of her cage and she soared off at once towards
a high tower which housed all the school owls.

THE OLDEST RECORDED MERPEOPLE WERE KNOWN AS SIRENS (GREECE) AND IT IS IN WARMER WATERS THAT WE FIND THE BEAUTIFUL MERMAIDS SO FREQUENTLY DEPICTED IN MUGGLE LITERATURE AND PAINTING.

—FANTASTIC BEASTS AND WHERE TO FIND THEM

A GAME BOOK

This "game book," dating from the early 17th century, was possibly made as a love token. The parchment has been folded into a concertina, with each section depicting an animal. A series of flaps overlays each portion of the manuscript, and can be opened or closed to create different types of creature. The game book includes mythical beasts such as dragons, manticores, and griffins, which can be transformed using the features of real animals such as monkeys, snakes, and lions. This mermaid can be given legs to become a woman or a man's head to become a fish-man. Although she appears different from the merpeople at Hogwarts, she is not to be trusted. The accompanying poem describes how the mermaid lured sailors, "Who leaving off their ship were found, On shore, by my enchantments drown'd."

▲
A GAME BOOK (ENGLAND, 17TH CENTURY)
British Library

THE GRAPHORN

This portrait of the aggressive Graphorn shows a large humped-back creature, with two horns and a heavy tail. According to Newt Scamander's *Fantastic Beasts and Where to Find Them*, the creature could be found in the mountainous regions of Europe. Olivia Lomenech Gill's evocative illustration shows how potentially dangerous J.K. Rowling's creation could be. The beast is shown scraping the ground with its "large, four-thumbed feet" ready to take on anyone foolish enough to stray too close. The artist has skillfully used highlights of color to add texture to the Graphorn's gnarled, grayish-purple skin.

▶

DRAWING OF THE GRAPHORN BY OLIVIA LOMENECH GILL
Bloomsbury

MOUNTAIN TROLLS CAN OCCASIONALLY BE SEEN MOUNTED ON GRAPHORNS, THOUGH THE LATTER DO NOT SEEM TO TAKE KINDLY TO ATTEMPTS TO TAME THEM AND IT IS MORE COMMON TO SEE A TROLL COVERED IN GRAPHORN SCARS.

—FANTASTIC BEASTS AND WHERE TO FIND THEM

THE SNALLYGASTER

▲
DRAWING OF THE SNALLYGASTER BY OLIVIA LOMENECH GILL
Bloomsbury

The Snallygaster is a creature of North American origin, said to have been named by Dutch settlers in the 1730s. The creature was added to the 2017 edition of *Fantastic Beasts and Where to Find Them*. Half bird, half serpent, the Snallygaster's name is derived from *schnell geiste*, a Pennsylvania Dutch term meaning "quick spirit." Despite its status as a mythological creature, numerous sightings of the flying beast have been reported in Frederick County, Maryland. *Valley Register*, a newspaper in Middletown, featured several stories from February to March 1909, describing the Snallygaster's enormous wings, long sharp beak, and fierce claws. The next recorded sighting occurred 23 years later. The last unsuccessful search for the Snallygaster took place in 1976.

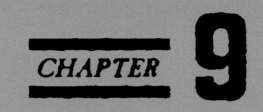

CHAPTER 9

PAST, PRESENT,

FUTURE

complexity of the later storylines, and how they were carefully intertwined. Employing the "series" method, the charts acted as early plotting aids for the author, with the titles and ordering of the chapters varying from the published versions. The plans also noted the whereabouts of individual characters—for example, Hagrid is "still with giants" for the first nine chapters—and the discovery of new information—Harry is at the Department of Mysteries when he realizes that prophecies are held there. In these plans, the secret Defense Against the Dark Arts organization is called the "Order of the Phoenix," while the official resistance is called "Dumbledore's Army."

▼
JACKET ARTWORK
FOR *HARRY
POTTER AND
THE ORDER OF
THE PHOENIX* BY
MARY GRANDPRÉ
Warner Bros.

NO	TIME	TITLE	PLOT	PROPHECY / Hall of Prophecy	Cho/Ginny	D.A.	O.O.T.P.	Snape/Harry+father	Hagrid+Grawp
13	OCT	Plots and Resistance	Harry, Ron & Hermione go to Hogsmeade, meet Lupin and Tonks — café talk, Umbridge tearing pass out — they recruiting for O.O.P. Hagrid frozen by in-laws	Harry sees Vol still formulating his plans. Wants to get into the DES who is set in t	Cho in Hogsmeade — wants to join O.O.P.	Tonks + Lupin	recruiting	Harry lesson slipping — to recruit for O.O.P	Hagrid still beaten up — Harry need — "he's feeder tidying that's not his advice"
14	NOV	The Order of the Phoenix	first meeting of the Order of the Phoenix	Senses smoke on Scar	Cho + Ginny both present	Umbridge now second	First meeting	Harry still slipping Snape not going	
15	NOV	The Dirtiest Tackle	Quidditch versus Malfoy. Harry	Nagini attacks Mr W.	Cho now madly in love		firehead ↑		
16	NOV	Black Marks	Row 16: skipping Snape lessons — Harry really in dog house as he only	Nagini got in, Vol has confirmation of Bode's story — only he + Harry can touch the prophecy	Cho kiss? Ginny/Grawp worried about father	Ron + rest of us called in to be told of father's injury	reactions — another meeting? overview	Row about Harry not Grawp	Hagrid sets up setup injuries
17	DEC	Rita Returns	Snape lesson Hogsmeade / Xmas shopping they meet Rita	Rita information 'Missy' slipkiss	Harry now considering Cho a bit — Ginny + S.O. clue?		O.O.P	Another lesson	Hagrid hospital wing
18	DEC	St. Mungo's Hospital for Maladies and Injuries	St Mungo's visit Xmas eve — see Bode (Macnair visiting) — Lockhart — see N —	NOW VOL IS ACTIVELY TRYING TO GET HARRY TO H.Q.P —	Ginny Dad	around			
				Bode dead — H.O.P again —	Harry + Ginny + Grawp Ron gets away		X. Vi Vi i Prog permission		
19	DEC	(Xmas)	Harry misses match v. Hufflepuff Order of Phoenix now suspected by Umbridge 2	Harry fighting short			O.O.P his meeting	Snape learn H can mention H.O.P prophecy	Hagrid out of hospital now goes into forest with Grawp — etc
20	JAN	Extended Powers of Elvira Umbridge	with Cho — Hogsmeade — Theke may not — Fleur replaces in week of	successful but not	Valentine date with Cho — v. miserable — then could row.	lift to keep	O.O.P	?	
21	FEB	(Valentines day)	Rita reports back on Bode etc Snape lesson			lift to keep Snape + Lupin	O.O.P	Snape goit eye but Harry became the stud do?	
22	FEB	Cousin Grawp	Umbridge now really going for Hagrid — firenze teaching — he'll go to prophecy + prophecies — Wan Hagrid or Umbridge meet Grawp	Harry stating he set it — blackest none	Cho wants back with Harry — maybe row	Grawp head	good	Snape Timothy approaches his	
23	MARCH	(Treason)	Castro — disarming of O O T P — Dumbledore takes the rap XX — Azkaban			firehead	see plot Meeting	↓	
24	APRIL	(Careers) (Guidance)	Careers consultation — Anon Order of Phoenix continues — Ginny has climbed as the wall in temper. Snape lesson	Harry starting to get it				Hagrid climbing into school re abandon Grawp

Handwritten planning grid (two tables) — J.K. Rowling's plan for *Order of the Phoenix*.

NO.	TIME	TITLE	PLOT	PROPHECY	CHO/GINNY	D.A.	O.P.	Harry/Dad/Snape	Hagrid + Group
1	Aug	Dudley Demented	Harry desperate for information – Contact – letters circumspect – desperate to rejoin Weasleys – Listens to news – sent Dudley showdown – meets Dementors – Mrs. Figg	→ but badly informed – think anyone can take – L.M. + Mac casing joint / Vol plotting Bode tries Imperius to put B. under Imperius					Still with giants
2	Aug	A Peck of Owls	Confused letters from Ministry – Harry to bed very worried – newspapers (D.P.s) 'Missy' Slipkiss	"				Mention of Snape obliquely by Aunt P.	Still with giants
3	Aug	The Auror's Guard	Moody, Tonky and Lupin turn up to take Harry to Grimmauld. Finish on entry to kitchen	" / announce rental of small room in D.A.					Still with giants
4	Aug	12. Grimmauld Place	(Percy) F+G plan? – Diggory + masses of information 'Missy Slipkiss' → Sirius explains Fudge's standpoint. Ginny cheeky + funny Mrs. W worried House-elf George + V. * Hermione	LM do put Bode/anyone from Dept Myst under Imperius if get chance	See plot	Meet for 1st time – explicit aims		Snape not present hint why	Still with giants
5	Aug	The Ministry of Magic	Interrogation – Mrs. Figg witness – Dumbledore too See entrance (Percy) Dept. of Mysteries	LM hangs around Min. on excellent terms with Fudge (puts Bode under)		still around			Still w. giants
6	Aug	Mrs. Weasley's Worst Fears	The clock – Mrs. W's premonitions of doom – (Percy etc) – 'Missy' S? ... More info + House-elf Hermio... discussion	Bode is under/and under orders to proceed v. cautiously	Ginny here Ginny/Hermione/Tonks	around Sirius farewell until xmas			Still with giants

NO	TIME	TITLE	PLOT	PROPHECY	Cho/Ginny	DA	OP	Snape/Harry/Father	Hagrid + Group
13	OCT	Plots + Resistance	Harry skips Snape lesson to go to Hogsmeade – Umbridge failing – pass note. MRH Recruiting for OP – Meg fresh injuries – Mann wants to incorporate SPEW in OP Daily Prophet story re: Dumbledore?	Harry sees Hall of P 1st time – Not sinister – beautiful. Vol still plotting –	Cho wants to join OP	Tonks + Lupin	Recruiting	Harry skips Snape furious	New injuries ... Hem reckon feeding up...
14	NOV	The Order of the Phoenix – Dobby finds	first meeting – named – Umbridge now reading Mail – Heding attacks bad Snape lesson (skipped last)	can't fathom what went wrong with Bode – decides to send Nagini on	Cho + Ginny both present	Umbridge intercepting mail	1st meeting	Snape lesson?	
15	NOV	The Dirtiest Tackle	Quidditch v. Malfoy – Cedric taunt – (Harry wild – handed following foul – followed – sin? can't sleep – restless – Umbridge – Malfoy cohoots – finally falls asleep Sees Nag. attack Mr. Weasley	Nagini attacks Mr Weasley Vol sees Harry walking Vol sees Harry should have...	Cho + OP? adore OP? Harry tackle – Malfoy in love – Ginny pleased	Umbridge fixhead?			Hagrid lessons falling apart
16	real end NOV	Black holes	'Missy Slipkiss' reaction to Mr. Weasley's injury – Gryffindors angry at Harry some born. Fred + George? action? Hesm contacts Snape → Rita. OP meeting	Vol has explanation of Bode – Nagini saw wrong, not only more concerned in the prophecy can touch it need he must steal	Cho, Leavy what Harry fouled in fall – in love. Kiss? Ginny next Cho re: Dad	fixhead re: Arthur?	meeting	Snape lesson v.v.bad – Harry saw sinister/not unsafe had enough	Hagrid in bad way – Umbridge going
17	DEC	Rita Returns	Hogsmeade – Xmas shopping – meet Rita →	Rita info 'Missy' Slipkiss → Bargain struck	Harry now avoiding Cho a bit. Ginny + S.O. else? Seamus @ OP?		OP		Hagrid hosp way. Grubbly Plank back
18	DEC	St. Mungo's Hospital for Magical Maladies & Injuries	see Lockhart " Neville " Bode " Arthur " Macnair	Vol now playing Harry v. subtly. Sees H + P again. scar hurting only v. slightly. See own name?	Ginny + Dad	around Moody + eye?			"

* Scrimp not Sirius lament?
also about sad future?
Cristmas being ~~restor~~ made again?

NO	TIME	TITLE	PLOT	PROPHECY	Cho/Ginny	DA	OP	Kreacher/Snape/father	Hagrid + Grawp
7	SEPT	Night Mares	Journey to Hog's — Hagrid not ~~there~~ effort to speak to Ron? Cho on train — arrival + see Thestral Horses — ~~up to~~ Grubbly-Plank greets — no Hagrid up to castle for Sorting — no Hagrid # — Malfoy hex? Prefect corridor rows?	Bode learns we on same level as we can't do it	Cho speaks some ideas are glimmering			Hag still w. giants
8	SEPT	Danger + Denial	FEAST — Prof Umbridge introduced — her speech — D's contrasting speech —	Vol impatiently awaits Bode's week but it is difficult (Harm and visions?)					"
9	SEPT	Joyce Umbridge	Exam emphasis — McGonagall 1st — project conversation — promise of careers guidance to whole class — Hem + Ron given Prefect bathroom keys + privileges — 1st Umb + the Weasel ~~nastifying~~ Harried			Can write in guarded way into HRH — know who involved			
10	SEPT/OCT	Blackout	Weekend — careers pamphlets — starting to get annoyed with Umbridge — Quid. practice — Umbridge studying — scar — Dumbledore — Snape lessons set up.	Bode hurt — 'elementary mistake' Harry sees Vol's subsequent fury	Cho very attracted by scar-morbid — Ginny — practical	Bill says Madame Maxine was back for start of term		
11	OCT	[Closed mind]	Teslawing — Umbridge meddling — Snape lesson. Lights in H's hut Harry + co go — see — giants + general background — Hagrid badly injured — Umbridge news that work	Vol plotting — can't make fresh attempt too soon. suspicion. Harry reads of Bode's 'elementary mistake' — all connected with V's desire — told — DA learns Bode has been attacked	writing in guarded fashion	Snape + Harry 1st lesson	Hagrid returns badly injured with Grawp
12	OCT	Offense ~~Against~~ The Dark Arts	~~Graphic~~ row with Umbridge re: teaching methods and — Hagrid — Dumbledore — Umbridge knows? ? SLP — and ? Umbridge not put D — C — any? lesson — in from yearning	Vol concocting new plan — SLP doesn't realise Harry + he can see 2 views or in 13	Cho still more attracted but in marked way. Comfort Ginny	Idea for OP	Snape lessons continue	Mysterious injuries continue

NO	TIME	TITLE	PLOT	PROPHECY	Cho/Ginny	DA	OP	Snape/Harry/Father	Hagrid/Grawp
19	DEC ~~Xmas~~	(Xmas)		Bode dead. Hall of Prophecy again	Harm/Krum Ginny + ?Seamus	Big reunion			
20	JAN ~~XMAS~~	Extended Powers of ~~Joyce~~ Umbridge	Harry misses meeting — Hufflepuff — OP now suspected by Umbridge — why weren't they all @ meeting — Snape lesson — might say students can't specifically banned		Cho + Harry break on Cith?	Big meeting	Snape lesson ongoing ?	Hagrid out of Hogwarts going purposefully into forest armed with spikes etc
21	FEB ~~XMAS~~	(Valentine's Day)	Date with Cho in Hogsmeade — thoroughly depressing — row — Cho in tears — Harry joins HR, depressed, at Rita meeting — Rita itching for details of Harry's private life — back to Hog to see — dusk release of time	Harry learning — more fighting increasingly	miserable Valentine date — row	forehead got to	Snape lessons ongoing keep in view	Hagrid trying cooling up still
22	FEB	Cousin Grawp	Umbridge persecuting Hagrid. Firenze teaching prophecies + prophets — HRH go to have stiff disc with Hag — meet Grawp — nightmare waiting to happen	Strong visions but natural	Ginny speak Cho back wants Harry can't take +	keep cup in	OP overview	keep in view	They meet Grawp
23	MARCH	Treason	Easter — discovery of OP — Dumbledore takes the rap. Then to Azkaban I must swallow. I trust I am allowed first then toothbrush?" He comes back if the top lost DA — Tonks is keen + if not OP? DA	~~curiosity~~ ~~detection~~ curiosity 'echo of militating of against'	(Ginny ginny ?Grawp)			Hagrid trying to cheer up — job but skin of teeth
24	APRIL	Careers Guidance	Careers consultation — Auror — OP meeting — Ginny, Fred + George extremely defiant to U. — doubts well —	getting better Harry's trying to get it now. ? Rita comes out for Dumbledore in 'The Questioner'	Harry back with Cho at meeting Dumb. leaving has agreed	Well	overview mention of progress	Hagrid sacked Grubbly-Plank back again

▼ ▶

PLANS FOR
*HARRY POTTER
AND THE
ORDER OF THE
PHOENIX* BY
J.K. ROWLING
J.K. Rowling

No	Time	TITLE	PLOT	PROPHECY	Cho/Ginny	DA	OdP	Snape/ Harry/ father	Hagrid & Grawp
25	APRIL	James Potter's Worst Hour	Snape showing that he wont teach etc. Harry sees Snape's worst ~~memory~~ day in Pensieve – Snape wont teach any more.	Harry now at V's mercy	Ginny recipient of confidences	Sirius running all along	keep in view – meeting	See PLOT	Hagrid + Grawp continue (unseen) H wont give up on Grawp
26	APRIL	~~Event~~ ~~Ascendant~~ Ascendant	Hagrid sacked – misses lesson. Harry sees Lupin/Sirius in fire – long discussion re: his father. "That's what Ginny said" see Snape Fred + George expelled	still fighting	Cho not happy	in corridors V etc gone back to go to Grawp	Sirius furious with Snape	∅
27	MAY	Azkaban Breakout	Quid – F & G gone – Gryff flattened – Azkaban breakout – Rita	Now like speeded up film sees H of P where it is, close up on name, how to get in	Cho breaks it off				
28	JUNE	~~Grawp~~ Thestral Horses	Vol breaks through horses + Neville + Ginny	Vol has decided to go for it – ~~breakout~~ breakout from Azkaban – unfortunately for him, D goes too, in hot pursuit – distract Aurors, draw them away from prison. clear ↑					
29	JUNE	Dept of Mysteries	Entrance – death – love – Hall of P – no dying (?) but his name on Prophecy – arrival of DEs	~~final~~ new vision of ? dying in H of P	DOESN'T REALISE UNTIL THERE THAT THE HALL CONTAINS PROPHECIES				
30	JULY	Battle DEs ~~arrival S + Co~~	arrival S + Co (alerted by Snape) Harry under Prophecy S dies						

"IT WAS ABOUT FIVE YEARS TO FINISH THE FIRST BOOK AND TO PLOT THE REMAINING SIX BOOKS, BECAUSE THEY WERE ALREADY PLOTTED BEFORE THE FIRST BOOK WAS PUBLISHED."

—J.K. ROWLING IN CONVERSATION WITH CHRISTOPHER LYDON, *THE CONNECTION*, WBUR RADIO, OCTOBER 12, 1999

"THE WARLOCK'S HAIRY HEART"

This is an original handwritten draft of one of the stories for *The Tales of Beedle the Bard*. It is one of four wizarding fairy stories written by J.K. Rowling to accompany "The Tale of the Three Brothers," which Hermione reads aloud to Harry and Ron in Chapter 21 of *Harry Potter and the Deathly Hallows*. This draft outlines the plot and captures the essence of the story, but it was extended for the published version. The tale is another example of a wizard attempting to use Dark Magic to protect himself from human vulnerability. In the Harry Potter novels, love has its own powerful magic. By rejecting his heart and starving it of love, the warlock's heart becomes "savage" and leads him to tragedy. Professor Dumbledore notes that this kind of Dark Magic would not be possible outside of fiction.

They gambolled and preened
> Undignified and foolish, dependent on the whims of a woman.

> locked up his heart.

> His friends and his family, laughed to see him so aloof. (not knowing what he had done) 'All will change,' they prophesied, 'when he meets the right maiden.'

But the young men did not fall in love. All around him young men and women were raised to ecstasy or plunged to despair by the vagaries of desire and affection, but the warlock walked unscathed through their midst, a cold smile upon his handsome mouth. He cared naught for anyone or anything, and he was proud for his own untainted and uninjured heart, locked up safe in its enchanted box.

Now his friends began, first, to wed, and then to have children. More than ever he was pleased to think of his untainted and uninjured heart safe in its enchanted box. ... their hearts ... he told himself, ... with the demands of their brats!'

His father fell ill and died. He watched his mother weep for days, heard her speak of a broken heart. In vain did she ask him why he did not cry. But the warlock congratulated himself again on his heartless state, for he had escaped her suffering.

One day, soon after his father's death, a beautiful

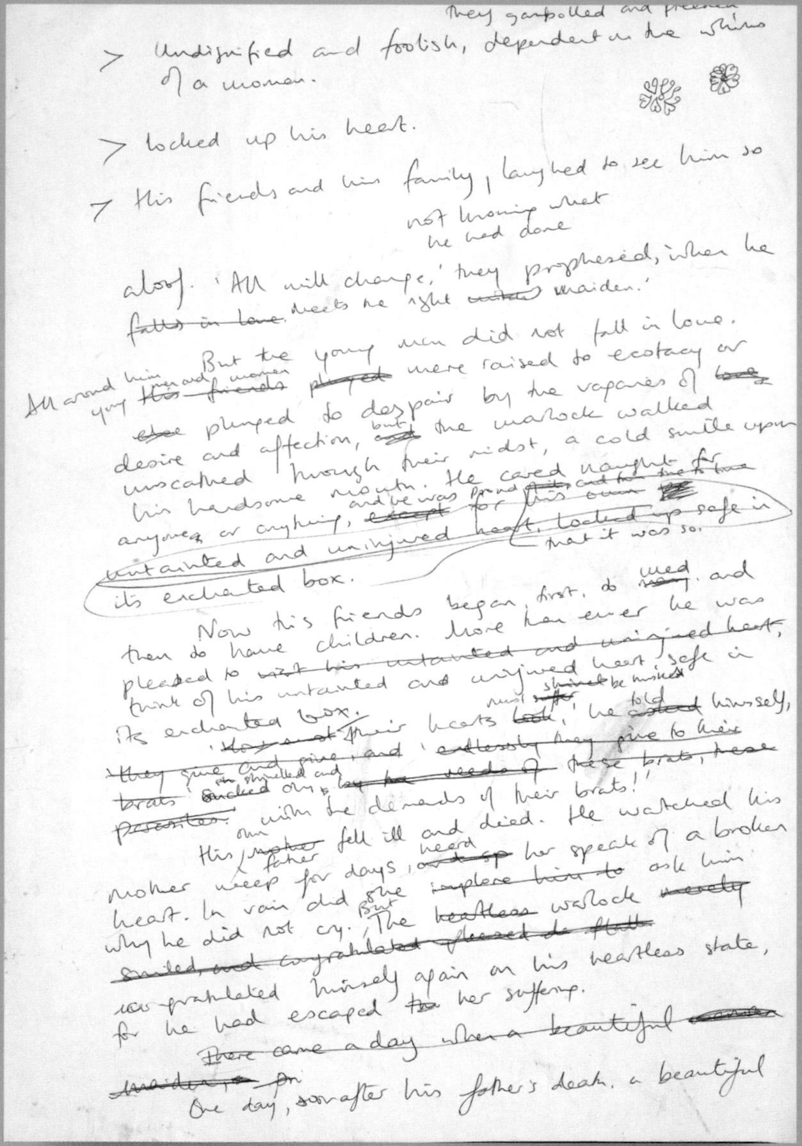

▲ ▶
DRAFT OF "THE WARLOCK'S HAIRY HEART" BY J.K. ROWLING
J.K. Rowling

Maiden ~~the~~ came to condole with the warlock's
mother ~~she was a most gifted~~ ~~this~~ ~~within~~
upon his father's death.
The young witch was beautiful, and gifted, ~~&~~ and her
family had much gold. The warlock had no ~~heart~~ to
feel, yet he ~~imagine~~ could understand the man
who ~~married~~ such a maid, ~~her~~ whose beauty would
excite envy in other men, whose magic could
~~assist a enable a ensure a comfortable life to~~
~~secure the comfort of her husband,~~ and ~~whose gold~~
~~me~~ assist her husband's ambitions and whose gold
would ensure his comfort. / Coldly and deliberately,
he began to pay court to ~~her~~ the maid. She was both
fascinated and frightened.
    "You seem not to feel," she said wonderingly.
~~"Have you a heart?"~~ "If I thought you truly had
                                    a heart..."
    The warlock understood that a show of feeling
was necessary to secure her hand, so he returned,
for the first time in ~~so~~ many years, to the place
where he had locked up his heart.
    ~~He had forgotten~~
    The heart was smaller by far than he
remembered, and much hairier. Nevertheless he
removed it ~~from~~ its enchanted ~~sights~~ box and
replaced it within his own breast.
    But the heart had grown savage during their
long estrangement. ~~He oppressed Anxious It knew desire without feeling~~
~~and through his veins there flowed lust within~~ It beat fast within him,
~~like poisoned wine spreading~~ and what it spread
He returned to the maid

J.K. ROWLING'S ANNOTATED *PHILOSOPHER'S STONE*

This unique first edition of *Harry Potter and the Philosopher's Stone*, with drawings and annotations by J.K. Rowling, was sold at a charity auction in aid of English PEN and Lumos in 2013. Forty-three of the pages have annotations or illustrations, among them reflections on and references to the Harry Potter series and films. In this copy, J.K. Rowling points out sections of text she refused to cut, and comments on an anomaly in Chapter 4 relating to snapped wands. She also describes the circumstances of the invention of Quidditch. On the first page, under the typeset title *Harry Potter and the Philsopher's Stone*, the author has written the simple words, "changed my life forever."

Harry Potter and the Philosopher's Stone

changed my life forever.

No shield here ~ crest. I mean that came in the later editions. But, frankly, bit of a monkey.

No shield here ~ crest. I mean

Perhaps Hufflepuff house would have the respect it deserves from fans if I'd stayed with my original idea of a bear to represent it?

HARRY POTTER

18

corner he stopped and took out the silver Put-Outer. He clicked it once and twelve balls of light sped back to their street lamps so that Privet Drive glowed suddenly orange and he could make out a tabby cat slinking around the corner at the other end of the street. He could just see the bundle of blankets on the step of number four.

'Good luck, Harry,' he murmured. He turned on his heel and with a swish of his cloak he was gone.

A breeze ruffled the neat hedges of Privet Drive, which lay silent and tidy under the inky sky, the very last place you would expect astonishing things to happen. Harry Potter rolled over inside his blankets without waking up. One small hand closed on the letter beside him and he slept on, not knowing he was special, not knowing he was famous, not knowing he would be woken in a few hours' time by Mrs Dursley's scream as she opened the front door to put out the milk bottles, nor that he would spend the next few weeks being prodded and pinched by his cousin Dudley ... he couldn't know that at this very moment, people meeting in secret all over the country were holding up their glasses and saying in hushed voices: 'To Harry Potter – the boy who lived!'

Harry Potter rolled over inside his blankets without wa

Professor McGonagall turned to Harry and Ron.

'Well, I still say you were lucky, but not many first years could have taken on a full-grown mountain troll. You each win Gryffindor five points. Professor Dumbledore will be informed of this. You may go.'

They hurried out of the chamber and didn't speak at all until they had climbed two floors up. It was a relief to be away from the smell of the troll, quite apart from anything else.

'We should have got more than ten points,' Ron grumbled.

'Five, you mean, once she's taken off Hermione's.'

'Good of her to get us out of trouble like that,' Ron admitted. 'Mind you, we *did* save her.'

'She might not have needed saving if we hadn't locked the thing in with her,' Harry reminded him.

They had reached the portrait of the Fat Lady.

'Pig snout,' they said and entered.

The common-room was packed and noisy. Everyone was eating the food that had been sent up. Hermione, however, stood alone by the door, waiting for them. There was a very embarrassed pause. Then, none of them looking at each other, they all said 'Thanks', and hurried off to get plates.

But from that moment on, Hermione Granger became their friend. There are some things you can't share without ending up liking each other, and knocking out a twelve-foot mountain troll is one of them.

This was the cut I refused to make -- my editor wanted to lose the whole troll-fighting scene. I'm glad I resisted

out that grubby little package. Had that been what the thieves were looking for?

As Harry and Ron walked back to the castle for dinner, their pockets weighed down with rock cakes they'd been too polite to refuse, Harry thought that none of the lessons he'd had so far had given him as much to think about as tea with Hagrid. Had Hagrid collected that package just in time? Where was it now? And did Hagrid know something about Snape that he didn't want to tell Harry?

Snape, brooding on the unfairness of life

"This wonderful treasure contains 21 original illustrations by the author. They include drawings of a swaddled Harry Potter on the Dursleys' doorstep, a menacing Professor Snape, an annotated sketch of the Hogwarts coat of arms, an Albus Dumbledore Chocolate Frog Card, Norbert the Norwegian Ridgeback, and the man with two faces."

JOANNA NORLEDGE
Curator

◄ ▲

HARRY POTTER AND THE PHILOSOPHER'S STONE, ILLUSTRATED AND ANNOTATED BY J.K. ROWLING (CA. 2013)
Private Owner

FANTASTIC BEASTS AND WHERE TO FIND THEM

This annotated screenplay of *Fantastic Beasts and Where to Find Them* contains J.K. Rowling's additions in her own handwriting. The screenwriting process is very different from writing a novel—it can be much more collaborative and require edits at almost any stage in the process of filming. The script must be technically filmable, and so the limits of imagination are potentially more restricted. Although *Fantastic Beasts* was J.K. Rowling's first screenplay, she did not appear to be confined by this new format. Filmmaker David Yates has talked about working on this script with her, describing how the author would rewrite, reinvent, and add astonishing detail to her characters and world, with seemingly no limit to her imagination. This draft represents the skeleton on which the film and the world of Newt Scamander were based.

▶

TYPEWRITTEN SCREENPLAY OF *FANTASTIC BEASTS AND WHERE TO FIND THEM* BY J.K. ROWLING, WITH AUTOGRAPH ANNOTATIONS
J.K. Rowling

"She has so much flowing through her head."

DAVID YATES,
on working with J.K. Rowling

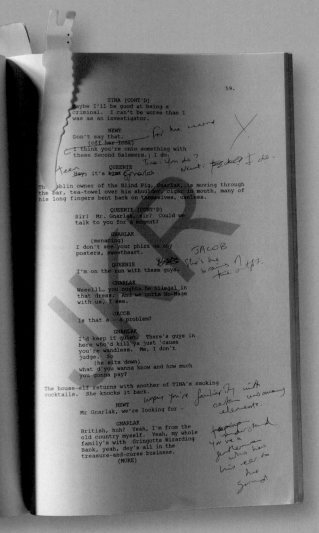

THE MACUSA
HEADQUARTERS

The Woolworth Building—the setting of the Magical Congress of the United States in the *Fantastic Beasts* movies—was the tallest building in the world when construction was finished in late 1912. Cass Gilbert, the architect, designed it in a gothic style that evokes the great European cathedrals. Gothic details can be found not only on the upper reaches of the skyscraper where gargoyles tower over the gables but also in the lobby where sculptures of fantastic creatures adorn the walls. The official opening of the "Cathedral of Commerce," as it was later called, occurred in April 1913 when President Woodrow Wilson flipped a switch from his White House office to activate the lights in the Woolworth Building. Electric lighting was relatively new at the time and was seen as a magical technological wonder.

▶

CASS GILBERT, STUDY FOR THE WOOLWORTH BUILDING (NEW YORK, 1910)
New-York Historical Society

FANTASTIC BEASTS OF NEW YORK

For over a century fantastic beasts have been keeping an eye on New Yorkers. This chimera—a fire-breathing monster with a lion's head—is one of eight from the 24th floor observatory of the Times Tower, the headquarters of the *New York Times*. Completed in 1904, the building was located in the heart of Times Square. In *Fantastic Beasts* the Square becomes a scene of chaos when an Obscurus unleashes its dark force over the city.

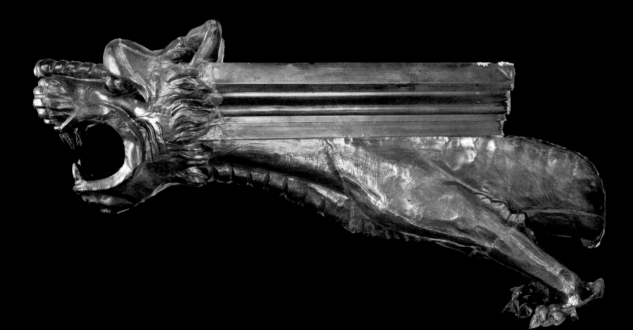

▲
CYRUS L.W. EIDLITZ,
GARGOYLE FROM THE TIMES
TOWER (NEW YORK, 1904)
New-York Historical Society

EERIE OWLS

If the adventurous and eccentric James Gordon Bennett Jr.—editor of the *New York Herald*,
America's highest circulating newspaper at the turn of the 20th century—had to choose
between bringing an owl, a toad, or a cat to Hogwarts he would have surely selected the first.
Bennett was so obsessed with owls that he allegedly kept live ones in his office and planned
his own mausoleum in the shape of an owl. In 1893 he commissioned architects McKim, Mead
& White to design a new headquarters in the style of a 15th century Venetian palazzo. Bennett
specified that the roof ledge be decorated with four-foot bronze owls, symbols of the wisdom
of the written word. The owls were even fitted with electric green glass eyes that eerily
glowed with the toll of the building's clocks.

HARRY POTTER AND THE CURSED CHILD

Based on an original new story by J.K. Rowling, Jack Thorne, and John Tiffany, *Harry Potter and the Cursed Child* is a play by Jack Thorne, produced by Sonia Friedman Productions, Colin Callender, and Harry Potter Theatrical Productions. It had its official premiere at the Palace Theatre, London, on July 30, 2016, and opened on Broadway in spring 2018 at the fully renovated Lyric Theatre on 43rd Street. In addition to receiving the 2017 Olivier Award for Best New Play and the 2018 Tony® Award for Best Play, set designer Christine Jones was honored with both the Olivier Award for Best Set Design and the Tony Award for Best Scenic Design of a Play for her work on the production.

This model for the Broadway production shows an evocative and flexible set design, which is integral to the theatrical magic that takes place onstage. Models such as this one help the creative team to work out the crucial detail of staging a play—ultimately making Harry Potter's world come alive before the audience's eyes.

In New York, designers Christine Jones and Brett J. Banakis had the privilege of not only building *Cursed Child*'s world on stage, but also the opportunity to redesign the entire Lyric Theatre, taking inspiration from the theater's original architecture as well as the Palace Theatre in London and elements of the set design itself, creating an entirely immersive experience from the moment the audience steps through the doors.

"This set model designed by Christine Jones and Brett J. Banakis includes steel arches reminiscent of familiar London train stations. The versatile set walls have rich wooden paneling and a beautiful round clock in the center. This design is rich in symbolism and Harry Potter heritage."

JOANNA NORLEDGE
Curator

▲

CHRISTINE JONES PRESENTING THE *HARRY POTTER AND THE CURSED CHILD* MODEL TO THE ORIGINAL WEST END COMPANY DURING REHEARSALS

▲
MODEL DESIGNED BY
CHRISTINE JONES WITH
BRETT J. BANAKIS,
AND BUILT BY MARY
HAMRICK, AMELIA COOK,
ARAM KIM, AND KYLE
HILL

◄
LYRIC THEATRE
AUDITORIUM DESIGNED
BY CHRISTINE JONES
AND BRETT J. BANAKIS,
PROJECT DIRECTED BY
GARY BEESTONE

For the 20th anniversary of the publication of *Harry Potter and the Sorcerer's Stone* in the United States, Scholastic commissioned Brian Selznick—author and illustrator of Caldecott Medal–winning *The Invention of Hugo Cabret*—to reimagine the cover art for the entire Harry Potter series. Selznick designed the seven covers as a single image that tells the story of the Boy Who Lived from his arrival on Privet Drive to the Battle of Hogwarts. The dynamic cover art is packed with details including the menacing dementors surrounding Harry's Patronus; magical creatures like Hedwig, Aragog, and a centaur; dramatic locations such as the Maze in the Triwizard Tournament; charmed objects including Hermione's Time-Turner and Harry's Invisibility Cloak; and the Hogwarts Express with a new generation of wizards on board.

INDEX OF
EXHIBITS
and
CREDITS

ABOUT J.K. ROWLING

J.K. Rowling is the author of the record-breaking, multi-award-winning Harry Potter novels. Loved by fans around the world, the series has sold over 500 million copies, been translated into over 80 languages, and made into 8 blockbuster films. She has written three companion volumes in aid of charity: *Quidditch Through the Ages* and *Fantastic Beasts and Where to Find Them* (in aid of Comic Relief and Lumos), and *The Tales of Beedle the Bard* (in aid of Lumos), as well as a screenplay inspired by *Fantastic Beasts and Where to Find Them*, which marked the start of a five-film series to be written by the author. She has also collaborated on a stage play, *Harry Potter and the Cursed Child Parts One and Two*, which opened in London's West End in the summer of 2016 and on Broadway in spring 2018. In 2012, J.K. Rowling's digital company Pottermore was launched, where fans can enjoy news, features, and articles, as well as original content from J.K. Rowling. She is also the author of *The Casual Vacancy*, a novel for adult readers, and the Strike crime series, written under the pseudonym Robert Galbraith. She has received many awards and honors, including an OBE and Companion of Honour, France's Légion d'honneur, and the Hans Christian Andersen Award.

THE CURATORS

JULIAN HARRISON

Julian Harrison is the lead curator of the British Library exhibition *Harry Potter: A History of Magic*. He is a specialist on medieval and early modern manuscripts, and previously curated major exhibitions on Magna Carta (The British Library, 2015) and William Shakespeare (The Library of Birmingham, 2016). He writes for and edits the British Library's Medieval Manuscripts Blog, which was named UK Arts and Culture Blog of the Year in 2014.

ALEXANDER LOCK

Alexander Lock is Curator of Modern Archives and Manuscripts at the British Library and cocurator of the exhibition *Harry Potter: A History of Magic*. He is a specialist of modern historical manuscripts and was lead researcher for the exhibition *Magna Carta: Law, Liberty, Legacy* (The British Library, 2015). His most recent book, *Catholicism, Identity and Politics in the Age of Enlightenment*, was published by Boydell and Brewer in 2016.

TANYA KIRK

Tanya Kirk is the British Library's Lead Curator of Printed Heritage Collections, 1601–1900, and a cocurator of *Harry Potter: A History of Magic*. She is a specialist in rare books and English Literature and has curated six literary exhibitions, including *Shakespeare in Ten Acts* (2016) and *Terror and Wonder: The Gothic Imagination* (2014/15). She is the editor of two collections of ghost stories, *The Haunted Library* (2016), and *Spirits of the Season* (2018). Like Dumbledore, she is very fond of knitting patterns.

JOANNA NORLEDGE

Joanna Norledge is Lead Curator of Contemporary Literary and Creative Archives and cocurator of the British Library exhibition *Harry Potter: A History of Magic*. She is a trained archivist and specialist in literary and theatrical archives at the British Library.

MARGARET K. HOFER

Margaret K. Hofer is Vice President and Museum Director at the New-York Historical Society, and project director for its presentation of *Harry Potter: A History of Magic*. As the Historical Society's decorative arts curator for more than two decades, Margi curated numerous exhibitions, including *Making It Modern: The Folk Art Collection of Elie and Viola Nadelman* (2016), *Stories in Sterling: Four Centuries of Silver in New York* (2011), and *A New Light on Tiffany: Clara Driscoll and the Tiffany Girls* (2007).

CRISTIAN PETRU PANAITE

Cristian Petru Panaite is Assistant Curator of Exhibitions at the New-York Historical Society, and coordinating curator for its presentation of *Harry Potter: A History of Magic*. An interdisciplinary humanities scholar, he most recently curated the major retrospective exhibition *Tattooed New York* (2017) and co-curated *Rebel Spirits: Robert F. Kennedy and Martin Luther King Jr.* (2018).

THE BRITISH LIBRARY

The British Library is the national library of the United Kingdom and one of the world's greatest research libraries. The library's collection has developed over 250 years—it exceeds 150 million separate items representing every age of written civilization. Its vast archive includes books, journals, manuscripts, maps, stamps, music, patents, photographs, newspapers, and sound recordings in all written and spoken languages. Among the greatest treasures in the library's collection are two copies of Magna Carta from 1215, the Lindisfarne Gospels, Leonardo da Vinci's notebook, the first edition of *The Times* from March 18, 1788, manuscripts of the Beatles' song lyrics, and the recording of Nelson Mandela's speech given at his trial. The oldest items in the collection are Chinese oracle bones that date back over 3,000 years—the most recent are today's newspapers and websites.

THE NEW-YORK HISTORICAL SOCIETY

The New-York Historical Society, founded in 1804, is dedicated to revealing the dynamism of American history and its influence on the world today through exhibitions, public programs, online outreach, and research. As New York's oldest museum and an internationally renowned research library, New-York Historical is a preeminent center for new humanities scholarship and leading provider of lifelong history education. Its holdings include 14 million documents, works of art, artifacts, and ephemera that span four centuries of American history and comprise one of the world's greatest collections documenting the history, culture, diversity, and continuing evolution of New York and the nation. Museum collections highlights include: John James Audubon's 435 unique watercolors for *The Birds of America*; renowned Hudson River School landscapes; and one of the most comprehensive collections of Tiffany lamps in the world. Artifacts relating to New York's participation in local and global events, among them the slave trade, the American Revolution, and the terrorist attacks on the World Trade Center, chronicle the history of New York and the nation. One of only 20 members of the Independent Research Libraries Association, New-York Historical's Library collections are strong in colonial history; the Revolutionary War; American military and naval history; the Anglo-American slave trade and conditions of slavery in the United States; the Civil War; and American biography and genealogy. In 2015, New-York Historical dramatically enhanced its holdings with the acquisition of the complete institutional archives of Time, Inc.—an extraordinary record of the 20th century.

9 Or.11390, f. 57v
50 IA.5209
51 IB.344
59 7511.c.30
64 Harley MS 3469, f. 4r
65 Additional MS 25724, f. 50v
67 Additional MS 17910, ff. 13v–14r
69 8905.a.15
81 1001/42
86-87 Harley MS 5294, ff. 21v–22r
88-89 Sloane MS 4016, ff. 37v–38r
90 452.f. 2
91 449.K.4(2)
94 Or.13347B, ff. 6v–7r
97 Harley MS 3736, ff. 58v–59r
98 Or.3366, f. 144v
113 Additional MS 36674, f. 10r
120 Additional MS 32496, f. 40r
121 1078.i.25.(5.)
122 Papyrus 46 (5)
123 Royal MS 12 E XXIII, f. 20r
124 Or 11390, between ff.6-7
130-131 Or.8210/S.3326
132-133 Cotton MS Tiberius C I, f. 28r
137 48.f. 7
139 Arundel MS 263, f. 104r + f. 107v
140-141 Maps C.44.a.42. (2.)
150 117.d.44.(2.)
154-155 Or.4830, ff. 20–21
156 YA.1988.a.9195
160 Royal MS 12 C XII, ff. 106v–107r
162 C.194.a.825.(2.)
166 8633.c.9
167 8633.eee.31
173 3835.c.26
175 Royal MS 12 C XIX, f. 67r
176 43.k.3–10
183 Additional MS 82955, f. 129r
184 1256.d.9
185 435.h.6
187 16084.d.15
188 Or.12859
189 Or.9178
190-191 Or.11390, ff. 57v–58r
206 38.g.10
212 460.c.1
213 505.ff. 16
217 C.7.d.7
218-219 461.b.11.(1.)
222 37.h.7
223 Burney MS 97, f. 18r
225 Harley MS 4751, f. 45r
226 G.10992
227 Additional MS 15241, f. 64r
235 Additional MS 57312

THANK YOU

With thanks to J.K. Rowling for the use of items from her personal collection; Jim Kay, Mary GrandPré, Brian Selznick, and Olivia Lomenech Gill for allowing us to use their artwork; Emily Clement, David Saylor, Gabriel Rumbaut, and Joe Romano from Scholastic; Robert Davies, Abbie Day, and Sally Nicholls from British Library Publishing; Dayna Bealy, Eleanor Gillers, Jill Reichenbach, and Glenn Castellano from the New-York Historical Society; and Ross Fraser from The Blair Partnership.

This book was designed by Rodrigo Corral Studio. The type was set in ITC Cheltenham, designed by Tony Stan. The display type was set in Windsor, created by Eleisha Pechey.